"*A Journey Worth Taking* is a winsome invitation to take seriously the mystery of your life. 'Why am I on this earth?' may be one of the most important questions you can ponder if you want to live a life of more than quiet desperation or cul-de-sac mediocrity. Charles Drew calls us to the glory we can know and the beauty we can author if we heed the invocation to live into the story written for us to reveal. This is a book for any person of any age who is courageous enough to ask: how shall I live?"

Dan B. Allender, Ph.D.
President, Mars Hill Graduate School
Author, *To Be Told, The Healing Path,* and *The Wounded Heart*

"In *A Journey Worth Taking*, Charles Drew has written a well-researched, thought-provoking guide which offers a meaningful analysis of the unique stages of calling. A highly recommended read for anyone who has ever wondered, 'Why am I here?' "

Jane Hyun
Leadership Strategist and Executive Coach
Author, *Breaking the Bamboo Ceiling*

"I was moved to tears by this beautifully written, honest, and comprehensive perspective on life calling. Charles Drew presents a realistic but hopeful view—one solidly grounded in the reality of the triune God. This is a great book for anyone wanting to reflect on the purpose and direction of his or her life's work."

Chris Keidel
InterVarsity Christian Fellowship
Metro Philadelphia/Delaware Area Director

"Charles Drew has given us a great book to give away—especially to those who want a purpose-driven life and want to dig more deeply into the mysteries of that purpose. It is at once clear, personal, culturally up-to-date, and theologically rich—a perfect combination. Drew takes us a step beyond the literature that is presently available on the subject. Highly recommended."

Dr. Timothy Keller
Senior Minister and Founding Pastor
Redeemer Presbyterian Church
New York, NY

"In this deeply theological and intensely practical and encouraging book, Charles Drew offers each of us the realistic hope of one day being greeted by our Maker with the words, 'Well done, my good and faithful servant.' I can imagine no greater affirmation of the cosmic significance of human life on earth! I recommend this book to anyone who is wrestling with questions of identity and calling today."

Mardi Keyes
Co-Director, L'Abri Fellowship in Southborough, MA
Author, *Feminism and the Bible*
Contributor, *Women and the Future of the Family*

"This book rightfully places calling in the grand framework of eternity while bringing God down into the flesh of our very human lives. An understanding of the thoughts laid out here will lead to a life shot through with joy even in this fallen world."

Diane Langberg, Ph.D.
Psychologist
Author, *Counsel for Pastors' Wives* and *On the Threshold of Hope: Opening the Door to Healing for Survivors of Sexual Abuse*

"Find a group of others who are seeking direction in life and read this book together. The questions at the end of each chapter are worth the price, and you'll find yourselves drawn into a dialogue that will change your life."

The Rev. Peter C. Moore, D.D.
Dean and President Emeritus, Trinity Episcopal School for Ministry
Director, FOCUS, Inc.
Author, *Disarming the Secular Gods, A Church to Believe In,* and *Can a Bishop Be Wrong?*

A Journey Worth Taking

Finding Your Purpose in This World

Charles D. Drew

P U B L I S H I N G
P.O. BOX 817 • PHILLIPSBURG • NEW JERSEY 08865-0817

Unless otherwise indicated, all Scripture quotations are from the HOLY BIBLE, NEW INTERNATIONAL VERSION®. NIV®. Copyright © 1973, 1978, 1984 by International Bible Society. Used by permission of Zondervan Publishing House. All rights reserved.

Scripture quotations marked KJV are taken from the King James Version.

Scripture quotations marked ESV are taken from *The Holy Bible, English Standard Version*. Copyright © 2000, 2001 by Crossway Bibles, a division of Good News Publishers. Used by permission. All rights reserved.

Italics within Scripture quotations indicate emphasis added.

Page design and typesetting by Lakeside Design Plus

Printed in the United States of America

Library of Congress Cataloging-in-Publication Data

Drew, Charles D., 1950-
    A journey worth taking : finding your purpose in this world / Charles D. Drew.
        p. cm.
    Includes bibliographical references.
    ISBN 978-1-59638-042-4 (pbk.)
    1. Christianity—Essence, genius, nature. 2. Vocation—Christianity. I. Title.
BT60.D74 2007
248.4—dc22

                                                            2007012554

For Jeannie

My best and wisest human friend

Contents

Acknowledgments

This book is about living, and for that reason my deepest gratitude must go to those who have walked most closely with me through the years. I first want to thank my parents, Allen and Harriet ("Tootie") Drew, whose manner of living taught me to love creation and all that is in it, especially people—including myself. They also introduced me from my infancy to the church and therefore to God—a choice they made, despite their own doubts at the time, for the sake of their children.

I also want to thank my children, Allen and Sarah. Watching them grow into God-loving adults and shepherding them along the way have convinced me of the truth of what I try to say in these pages. They, together with their spouses, Heather and Peter, have been cheerleaders, enthusiastically sharing portions of the manuscript with friends and colleagues.

C. S. Lewis has done more for my "eschatological imagination" than any other thinker I have read, and the presence of his thought runs throughout the consummation section of this book. I am also indebted to Os Guinness, whose fine book, *The Call*, provided me with a number of vivid illustrations.[1]

Special thanks must go to David Powlison, who provided the (undeservedly) glowing foreword and offered some very helpful suggestions on the pacing and wording of the introduction. (I have shamelessly inserted large portions of his language into the text!)

I am also grateful to my friends at Emmanuel Presbyterian Church in New York City. The congregation responded so enthusiastically when I taught them this material at a retreat that I was persuaded to put it in writing. My elders have encouraged me to take time to write, and one of them, Earl Tai, carefully read through the manuscript, offering many helpful suggestions for tightening its argument. A number of our members have enriched the writing by permitting me to include portions of their own stories.

I especially thank Jeannie, my wife of thirty-five years, whose wisdom in the matters under discussion, application of them in life, and encouragement regarding the project have been impossible to measure adequately.

1. Os Guinness, *The Call: Finding and Fulfilling the Central Purpose of Your Life* (Nashville: Word Publishing, 1998).

Foreword

Have you ever learned a foreign language or watched someone else become fluent? When you think about it, the process is quite amazing. You repeat syllables that initially sound meaningless: *amo amas amat amamus amatus amant*. (That's about all I remember from seventh grade Latin, in which I remained decidedly non-fluent.) You labor mechanically to connect familiar meanings in your native tongue to unfamiliar words from the new language. You slowly start to put words together, and your initial sentences have all the profundity of "Dick said, 'Look Jane. See Spot run.'"

But something happens along the learning curve. Gradually, when the process works, as you immerse yourself in literature, in culture, or in conversation, a wonderful transformation occurs. You start to get the hang of it. It all begins to make sense. You're no longer making a tedious translation in your head. You find yourself beginning to read, to think, to dream, to answer spontaneously in new words. The world even looks and feels different when you can put it in different words.

This book bids to teach you a new "language" for thinking about your life and identity. It's not about *amo amas amat*, of course, or the Chinese or English equivalents. Perhaps we could say that it's in the universal language of reality. That's not our native tongue. It's in the language of indestructible hope. That's not how any of us naturally thinks. It's in the language of the one life purpose worth living for and dying for. They don't teach us that in school. Your life looks and feels different when you can put it in different words.

Charles Drew makes some astonishing promises. If this book were in tabloid form, it would contain headlines like these:

Find your true self!
Live a wonderful life!!
Begin a journey of self-discovery!!!

No exaggeration, Charles Drew fulfills exactly these promises. But he does so in a most surprising, sensible, and human way. You find your true self . . . as you stop thinking so much about yourself. You live a wonderful life . . . as you learn to do mundane things well. You discover yourself . . . as you discover someone who is far more fascinating than you. Inspirational pep talks, techniques, and strategies can never get you to any of these good places. Instead, you need *reasons*. And Charles Drew gives you reasons. Good reasons.

Those reasons deserve bold print and exclamation points. But I think you'll find that they sneak up on you quietly and take you by the hand. Listen well as you read. Think hard. Take it to heart. It will be a bit like watching as predawn darkness lightens and brightens into sunrise and then full day. A slow and quiet happening . . . mundane . . . and wonderful beyond telling when you think about it.

This is a book to take slowly, so it sinks in. You might even want to go back and reread the previous three paragraphs, so you'll know what you're getting into.

David Powlison, Ph.D.
Author of *Seeing with New Eyes*
and *Speaking Truth in Love*

You have made us for yourself, and our hearts are restless until they find their rest in you.

Augustine

Introduction

was in Penn Station in New York City on the Friday afternoon following 9/11. Always busy at the end of the week, the place was overwhelmingly so, since the government had shut down all the local airports for security reasons. Vast numbers of people were desperate to get out of the city, and Penn Station was one of the few ways out.

One of the desperate ones was a businessman who had just missed his train to DC only to discover that he had no chance of another seat until Sunday evening. Suitcase on wheels swerving behind him, he plowed furiously through the crowd screaming obscenities at a woman (presumably his wife) who seemed to be the reason for his misfortune.

As he was carrying on, something very different caught my ear. At first I could not identify it, but gradually I recognized it as applause. It began at the far end of the terminal and steadily grew until it filled the station. It was deep and sustained: not the raucous "hooting" variety of applause that erupts in Madison Square Garden when the New York Rangers score, but rather something the likes of which I had never heard in a public place. Mystified, I searched for its source, and when I discovered it, I understood. A company of firefighters was making its way through the terminal, presumably to the subway, to continue its trek to ground zero. I joined in the applause and wept as they passed by.

By summer 2002, record numbers of firefighters and police were retiring from their respective departments in New York City. I wonder whether one of the reasons is this: the immense social value attached to firefighting and police work because of 9/11 is not sustainable over time. In other words, many in these professions are beginning to experience a crisis of meaning now that the intense work is over and they are back to business as usual.

Business as Usual

"Business as usual" can be pretty dull, and we all face it much of the time. This is true whether we are changing diapers, doing research, preparing another lesson, trying to resolve another personnel spat at work, wrestling with another set of math problems for school, lingering "on call" at the fire station, or preparing another report for a client. Regardless of how we fill our hours, whether we get paid for what we do or volunteer, whether our work is recognized as "legitimate" by mainstream culture or not, we all struggle at times with the meaning of it all.

What adds to the dullness of "business as usual" is a widespread loss of meaning in modern culture. Professor Allan Bloom's 1987 portrait of students still applies:

> The souls of young people are in a condition like that of the first men in the state of nature—spiritually unclad, unconnected, isolated, with no inherited or unconditional connection with anything or anyone. They can be anything they want to be, but they have no particular reason to want to be anything in particular. Not only are they free to decide their place, but they are also free to decide whether they will believe in God or be atheists, or leave their options open by being agnostic; whether they will be straight or gay, or, again, keep their options open; whether they will marry and whether they will stay married; whether they will have children—and so on endlessly. There is no necessity, no morality, no social pressure, no sacrifice to be made that militates going in or turning away from any of these directions, and there are desires pointing toward each, with mutually contradictory arguments to buttress them. [1]

We enjoy unbridled freedom and seemingly unlimited options, but they exist in a social milieu that has no coherent "story." We are free to be ourselves, but we are fuzzy about who we are and how we fit in with what is going on around us. We lack vision, in other words, and because we lack vision we lack the passion we need to cut our way through the inevitable setbacks and frequent dullness in whatever we have set out to

1. Allan Bloom, *The Closing of the American Mind* (New York: Simon & Schuster, 1987), 87.

do. In the absence of a story that connects us to what is going on around us (and to other people), life grows lonely and its purpose often shrinks down to the hollow and even frantic pursuit of whatever pays the biggest dividends (emotionally, spiritually, or materially).

This book addresses our quest for meaning. It is a book about what people of an earlier age described as "calling"—about finding our place in the scheme of things. In the pages ahead we will address a number of related questions: How do we discover our calling? Should we expect our working lives to correspond to our callings, or is calling something deeper? If calling is deeper than work, does that make work essentially meaningless? If calling is deeper than work, does it make work little more than a means to something else? Do we, for example, study for no other reason than to get good grades; do we work hard at our jobs for no other reason than to get a promotion or more pay?

How are we to interpret the dreariness and frustration that so often beset our work? Are certain types of work inherently more valuable, or more spiritual, than others? Who determines the significance of our life work: Is firefighting significant only when Penn Station applauds firefighters? Is a career as a concert pianist worthwhile only if our parents and friends say it is? Or are we, and we alone, the ones who determine the value of our lives' direction? Should we abandon that path whenever our sense of purpose or satisfaction in that path begins to wane?

It won't be long before you discover that I am writing from a faith perspective. Please don't let that put you off if you are coming from a different place. I think you will see that crucial parts of what I have to say will resonate with your own life experience. And I hope you will find that the less familiar things also resonate—in a different way. A fresh understanding of your deepest experience can open up unsuspected opportunities for growth. You may even find yourself giving the Christian faith another (or first) look. One of the reasons I am a believer is that Christian faith "fits" life as it really is. Perhaps you will discover this yourself.

Four Big Ideas: Switchbacks on a Mountain Trail

We will address the questions surrounding life purpose in the context of four great ideas:

- Human life comes with built-in purpose.
- Something goes wrong with how we express our purpose.
- What gets ugly and destructive can be remade beautiful and right.
- What we do matters, because we are going somewhere.

If pursuing my life purpose is like trekking up a tall mountain, then these four ideas are like switchbacks along the way. A spectacular vision awaits me at the top, but I won't get there without following a trail that at times seems to double back on itself. Sometimes, for example, the great news that my life has a built-in purpose (idea one) may seem to be contradicted by the distressing news that something is terribly wrong with my efforts to express that purpose (idea two).

Let me put these realities together into one rather sinuous sentence. "Your life is not random . . . *but* it's not 'OK just the way it is' . . . *yet* you aren't hopelessly stuck . . . *and* what you do counts for much more than any of those momentary gains coming from instant gratification or ego gratification." These four ideas aren't contradictory or even paradoxical. They are switchbacks, like the turnings in a good story, a real-life story that is going somewhere. A clear-minded understanding of your life purpose (one that is both realistic and hopeful) has to take all four of these things into account.[2]

Here are the technical words for describing these four big ideas: creation, fall, redemption, and consummation. Chapter 1 paves the way for our discussion by making the case for a cosmos in which the notion of calling (and the Caller that it presupposes) makes sense. Chapter 2 defines calling as we will be using the term. Chapters 3 through 20 open up something of the meaning of the four "big ideas." The book concludes with a brief chapter offering some practical advice on next steps. The appendix tells the stories of a number of folks in my New York congregation, stories that will help illustrate how the "big ideas" work themselves out in real life.

At the end of each chapter you will find a series of questions or exercises. Their purpose is to help you internalize and apply the material in the chapter. You will find them useful for either individual reflection or group discussion.

2. I am indebted to David Powlison for the switchback metaphor and much of the language in the previous two paragraphs.

1

Staging Points

He has also set eternity into man's heart, yet so that he cannot find out what God has done from the beginning to the end.

Ecclesiastes 3:11

Is Anyone Calling?

Before we plunge into the questions outlined in the Introduction, we need to address a fundamental one: what sort of a universe do we live in?

The traditional notion of calling presupposes a Caller. That is, it assumes a Person who communicates intelligibly with us. There is little point in a book about calling if there is nobody at home in heaven or if he mumbles. We will assume his existence throughout the book. But why, you might reasonably ask, should we? The answer, in summary form, is this: the world as we actually experience it doesn't make sense without him.

Today's Fashionable Skepticism

A current fashion is to assume that all statements about God are in actual fact statements about the speaker. "G-o-d," in other words, is a three-letter symbol for talking about our religious feelings and hopes, our religious perspectives and fears and frustrations—all of which have arisen as a result of a complex assortment of evolutionary instincts, psychological needs, and cultural (including family) training.

When, for example, I say to a friend, "God loves you," I may think I am talking about the attitude of an eternal Person. But what I am really doing is using religious language to express my good will toward my friend and to encourage him in some way. Likewise, when I speak of God "calling," I am not really talking about a communication from an eternal Person. I am, rather, using a "feel good" expression that helps me cope with cosmic silence or, at best, cosmic fuzziness. So why not drop the "God thing" altogether and do your best, with some help from friends and mentors, to figure out what life means on your own?

Many in our day find this idea compelling. It sounds both humble (Who am I to tell someone else what life means?) and liberating (I'm free to find a life purpose that works for me).

But there are some problems. First, this approach is humble only if there is no God calling; but if there is, then it can be a ruse for avoiding him. C. S. Lewis said in *Surprised by Joy* that our search for God is often hardly different from the mouse's search for the cat. Second, this approach is not necessarily liberating. When, having abandoned the notion of a knowable Caller, we turn to creating our own reality, we will often find ourselves trapped in whatever people around us are saying. Or, if we are more independent types, we will tend to create a life direction that is ruled by whatever happens to suit our own preferences and needs—which means that we will be trapped inside ourselves.

Closed Box or Open?

And there is a larger problem. A major source of the skepticism we have been discussing is a particular belief about what is ultimately real—about what was there before we showed up. And this belief, if you press it, does not make sense of life as we actually experience it.

There seem to be only two possible answers to the question, What has always been here? The first answer—the one that feeds our skepticism about a real Caller—is this: matter (or energy) has always been around. That is to say, the highly concentrated stuff that exploded in what we call the big bang didn't appear out of nowhere. It has always been around in one form or another. According to this first view the cosmos is like a huge closed box, inside which everything, including atoms, ideas about what is good, and ideas about God, has its origin. Edward O. Wilson, Harvard biology professor, uses this language to explain the rise of our sense of right and wrong:

> [The evidence of biology and brain science] favors a purely material origin of ethics. . . . Causal explanations of brain activity and evolution, while imperfect, already cover the most

facts known about moral behavior with the greatest accuracy and the smallest number of free-standing assumptions.[1]

The second (and only other possible) answer is this: a personal God predated and produced matter (and energy). That is, at some point before the big bang, not even the highly concentrated stuff existed. There was nothing at all, except for God—an infinite and personal Being. In this case the cosmos is not itself eternal. It is rather like a huge God-built box which is open at the top, and into which God acts as he sees fit.

Neither of these views is provable—they are both expressions of faith. But the faith required to embrace the first view requires much more of a leap than the faith required to embrace the second. The idea of a "closed box" cosmos obliges us to believe a whole raft of things that simply don't make sense. Here are a few of the big ones:

- Love is ultimately just biology and social engineering: "I love you—let's marry" is more honestly rendered, "You've got good genes—let's mate and propagate the species."
- The universal human longing for meaning is itself meaningless.
- Beautiful music is nothing but the effect of certain patterns of electrical impulses on our brains, themselves stirred up by nothing but the working of certain patterns of sound waves on our eardrums.

1. Edward O. Wilson, *Consilience: The Unity of Knowledge* (New York: Vintage Books, 1999), 263.

- Our moral outrage at evil things (consider our response to the assault on the World Trade Towers or the Holocaust) has no grounding outside ourselves.

Such assertions are counterintuitive; they must be held despite deep and virtually universal human conviction and behavior. But if we take the other approach—if, in other words, we welcome a personal God (a God who loves and who is good and beautiful) into the picture, our quests for meaning, beauty, love, and goodness begin actually to make sense.

Let me illustrate. I had a friend in college named David who was a militant "closed box" type. During one of our discussions in our freshman year I asked him whether, given his view of ultimate reality, love was essentially chemistry. He said, "Yes!" and protested upon further questioning that this reality did not bother him.

Junior year David fell in love with Margaret. At an opportune moment I put the same question to him. This time there was some hesitation and consternation in his answer. David was not quite sure what to say. He found himself caught between his worldview and his experience. Though he did not change his worldview, I admired his willingness to admit the difficulty he had begun to encounter fitting his philosophy into life as he actually lived it.

A Faith That Fits

The recurrent and overwhelming need we have for meaning and love, the powerful intuitions we have about the reality of goodness and truth, the sense we have that beauty is an invitation to a reality that is bigger than the sum of its parts . . . such common human experiences do not prove a personal God. But they make much more sense in a God-originated universe than they do in the closed-box universe.

To speak of calling, then, is not to indulge in a coping mechanism in the face of a silent cosmos. Nor is it meant to suggest that we can easily figure God out (the Bible readily admits to both our selfishness and our limits—both of which hamper our discernment).[2] It is rather to give expression to a faith that sits well with the world in which we find ourselves living and acting. It sits well with what we all seem to know intuitively about the nature of things—that we are made for relationship, that we are accountable, and that our lives count. It receives encouragement from passages such as this one from Psalm 139:

> O Lord, you have searched me and you know me. You know when I sit and when I rise; you perceive my thoughts from afar. You discern my going out and my lying down; you are familiar with all my ways. . . . I am fearfully and wonderfully made; your works are wonderful, I know that full well. My frame was not hidden from you when I was made in the secret place. . . . All the days ordained for me were written in your book before one of them came to be. How precious to me are your thoughts, O God! How vast is the sum of them![3]

2. "What is man that you are mindful of him" (Ps. 8:4); "The heart is deceitful above all things" (Jer. 17:9). Note that these dark realities are matched and overturned, happily, by the grace of a God who loves us enough to make himself accessible to us and who is powerful enough to do so despite our blindness.
3. Ps. 139:1–3, 14–15a, 16a–17.

Questions
for Reflection and Discussion

1. Compare the "open box" universe with the "closed box" universe. Do you agree that it takes more faith to believe in the second than in the first? Why/why not?

2. How and where do people who believe in a closed universe find meaning in life and direction for their life work? (Make this real: think of people you know—perhaps yourself.) Discuss the strength and stability of the sources of meaning and direction you just identified.

3. Discuss the following statement:

   When, having abandoned the notion of a knowable Caller, we turn to creating our own reality, we will often find ourselves trapped in whatever people around us are saying. Or, if we are more independent types, we will tend to create a life direction that is ruled by whatever happens to suit our own preferences and needs—which means that we will be trapped inside ourselves.

4. What is "calling"? Try to come up with a full definition.

Come, all you who are thirsty, come to the waters; and you who have no money, come, buy and eat! . . . Listen, listen to me, and eat what is good, and your soul will delight in the richest of fare. Give ear and come to me; hear me, that your soul may live.

Isaiah 55:1a, 2b–3a

I have come that they may have life, and have it to the full.

Jesus, in John 10:10

2

What Is Calling?

n his best seller *What Should I Do with My Life?* Po Bronson talks about how he customarily responds to a frequently asked question:

> "So is your book about life, or about careers?" And I . . . laugh, and warn them not to get trapped by semantics, and answer, "It's about people who've dared to be honest with themselves."[1]

1. Po Bronson, *What Should I Do with My Life?* (New York: Random House, 2003), xix.

We are caught in a similar bind, for, whereas calling is (or may be) closely connected with career, the two are not identical. Calling is both larger and more complex than career. It carries through every season and circumstance of my life, and has more to do with *who* I am and with *how* I do what I do than with *what* I happen to be doing.

Calling comes from God, and he beckons at three levels, often simultaneously. First, he calls us to himself and to people (we will call this primary calling). Second, God calls us to self-discovery—that is, to the faithful and joyful expression of who we are (secondary calling). And third, God calls us to service—that is, to certain present tasks and duties that, in a fallen and imperfect world, simply need to be done (we will call this tertiary calling).

Called to God and People

Primary calling, which encompasses and gives life to the other two, is *calling to God and to people.* God calls us, in other words, to love him "with all our heart, soul, mind and strength" and to "love our neighbor as ourselves." According to the Bible, life at its deepest level is relational (or, to use the biblical word, *covenantal*).

For some strange reason people often don't get this. They think that the chief idea in the Bible is, "Behave and maybe you will get to heaven." But this is not true. The chief idea of the Bible is, "Come to me and live!" We find this notion everywhere in Scripture, as the following sampling of texts proves. In the first, God pleads with his people through Isaiah, begging them to find their deepest satisfaction in him. The second text, which gives us a window into the way Jesus prays for us, defines "eternal life" relationally. And the third, which takes us back to the dawn of human history, gives us God's assessment of solitary human life.

> Come, all you who are thirsty, come to the waters; and you who have no money, come, buy and eat! . . . Listen, listen to me, and eat what is good, and your soul will delight in the richest of fare. Give ear and come to me; hear me, that your soul may live.

> This is eternal life: that they know you, the only true God, and Jesus Christ, whom you have sent. . . . Father, I want those you have given me to be with me where I am. . . . I have made you known to them, and will continue to make you known in order that the love you have for me may be in them and that I myself may be in them.

> The LORD God said, "It is not good for the man to be alone. I will make a helper suitable for him."[2]

We are made for God, to discover and enjoy him, to be known and enjoyed by him. And we are made to know him in and through human community.

Everything in life points to this two-sided "primary" beckoning. To have God without people is lonely; to have people without God does not satisfy. We die inside, no matter how rich, powerful, and gifted we are, without relationships—the most important of which is our relationship to God. Food, shelter, MP3 players, satisfying work, beautiful possessions, good looks, athletic prowess and great intelligence, good families and strong marriages, well-ordered and just government: all these

2. Isa. 55:1a, 2b–3a; John 17:3, 24, 26; Gen. 2:18.

things, wherever they are found, come from God, and they invite us to look back through them to the One from whom "every good and perfect gift" comes.[3] And the inevitable loss, through selfishness and death, of life's good things reminds us that they were never meant to satisfy.

Wiring and Necessity

Secondary calling is more specific than primary. It is *calling to self-discovery*—to the faithful and joyful expression of who I am. God wants me to know myself so that I can bring all that I am—my abilities, my enthusiasms, my loves, my training, and my opportunities—to the business of living. And he wants me to use all that I am to bring order and goodness and beauty to the life I have been given—to time, to space, to thinking, to possessions, to relationships. He wants me, in short, to be a faithful steward.

Secondary calling can relate to career, but it is not the same thing (no matter how much we may love what we do for a living). It is perhaps best identified with my God-given "name."

God does a lot of naming in the Bible, and the naming often signals a person's unique contribution to God's purposes or joy. Jesus changes Simon's name to Peter (which means "rock") and adds, "On this rock I will build my church." God commands Mary and Joseph to name their son "Jesus" (or "Joshua," which means "Yahweh saves") and explains, "because he shall save his people from their sins."[4] And lest we think that such naming is only for special people, we have

3. James 1:17.
4. Matt. 16:18; Matt. 1:21.

Jesus' remarkable promise in Revelation 2:17 to every faithful follower: "To him who overcomes, I will . . . give him a white stone, with a new name written on it, known only to him who receives it."

A new, mysterious, and beautiful name awaits each of us. But the Lord is already at work giving us glimpses of it as we answer his call day to day.

The sad thing about secondary calling is that most people in our broken world have little opportunity to pursue it. Most people spend their days simply surviving—doing what is necessary to keep themselves sheltered and fed (more about this later).

Necessary Tasks

Tertiary calling is to service—that is, *a calling to do certain necessary tasks that, in a fallen and imperfect world, simply need to be done.*[5] These tasks may not correspond in some obvious way to my particular gifts (that is, to my secondary calling). They rather arise simply because love demands that they be done and we happen to be on hand at the moment to do them. Few people, for example, feel "called" to change diapers or set up chairs for weekly worship in a rented facility, nor does changing diapers or setting up chairs require extraordinary "gifting." Nevertheless, love requires that such things be done and that the burden of doing them be shared. Jesus no doubt swept out the carpentry shop from time to time, and so must we.[6]

---

5. Gordon Smith speaks of what I am calling "tertiary calling" in *Courage and Calling* (Downers Grove, IL: InterVarsity, 1999), 10.

6. "Carry each other's burdens, and in this way you will fulfill the law of Christ" (Gal. 6:2). "Now that I, your Lord and Teacher, have washed your feet,

An Inseparable Relationship

These three levels of calling cannot be separated from one another (they all come from the same Person), though at times one may appear more dominant than the others. The odd thing about the calls to self-discovery and service (secondary and tertiary calling), for example, is that in our upended and oppressive world we may find ourselves spending more time and energy on the latter than on the former. This is George Bailey's problem in the film *It's a Wonderful Life*. He keeps putting off his dream to "get out of town" in order to meet the needs of family and friends. His frustration mounts until a crisis drives him nearly to suicide. What saves the day is the visit from Clarence, the apprentice angel, who opens George's eyes to what life would be like had George never been born. The film shows how the call to service can seem sometimes to swallow up the call to self-discovery.

Thankfully, the film also reminds us that the call to serve is easily as weighty as the call to develop one's gifts, and pays huge dividends to those of us who heed it. We can put this even more strongly: the most effective way to pursue self-discovery (secondary calling) is to serve (tertiary calling). In other words, if I set out to discover myself, my search will be frustrating. If, on the other hand, I set out to serve, I will begin to discover things about myself along the way.

First Things First

What ties all calling together is the Caller—which is why primary calling must always be primary. We must never, in

---

you also should wash one another's feet. . . . No servant is greater than his master" (John 13:14, 16).

other words, allow work (often an element of secondary calling) or even service to eclipse love for God and people. Whether I am praying, closing a deal, doing a math problem, blocking a punt, disciplining a child, volunteering at a homeless shelter, sharing my faith, or enjoying a symphony, every act is done before him and in response to him.

The question I must ask as I consider a career in banking is the same question I must ask as I consider a career as a missionary: where, Lord, can I best discover you and serve people? And the question I must ask as I volunteer at church is the same one I must ask as I change a diaper or prepare a report at work: "Is God my joy as I work?" "Pursuing my vocation" does not, rightly, mean "working hard at my job." It rather means "enjoying God and loving people as I seek faithfully to use my gifts and opportunities to his glory."[7] The Westminster Shorter Catechism reminds us, "The chief end of man is to glorify God and to enjoy him forever," an impossible pursuit for those who have made gods of their work.

I have a good friend who is an actor. She spoke to me once from London's West End, where she was doing a show, about her conversations with a searching actor friend. They had been able to talk about the Lord, and she said to me, "I wonder if the main reason God brought me here was so that I could spend all this time with Tricia." By this she did not mean that life is all about evangelism. (She loves the theater, is good at it, and works very hard at it—seeing it as a calling from God.) She meant that life is all about love, and that self-discovery and self-expression must never be isolated from service to people and God. She had her priorities right.

7. "Whatever you do, do it all for the glory of God" (1 Cor. 10:31).

When we allow the calls to self-discovery and service to eclipse the call to God, they cease to be calling at all, for we have bidden the Caller to leave. We become idolaters (even if we are engaged in worthwhile spiritual causes), and our idolatry makes us miserable. Self-discovery becomes depressing because the things we "discover" about ourselves tend to be unflattering. Work and service begin to dry up and lose their sense of purpose. Or they degenerate into what we do to get approval or to get the money we need to enjoy ourselves somewhere else. Or they become obsessions that bring on sleepless nights, inhibit serious friendships, and send us to an early grave (more about this later in the book).

Patience Required

Let me make one last observation: calling in both the primary and secondary senses (the senses that will occupy most of our discussion) unfolds over a lifetime—and beyond. This is so because of who God is and because of who we are.

God is infinitely great and beautiful. We will take eternity to discover him:

> Can you fathom the mysteries of God? Can you probe the limits of the Almighty? They are higher than the heavens— what can you do? They are deeper than the depths of the grave—what can you know? Their measure is longer than the earth and wider than the sea.[8]

One of the tragedies for those raised in the church is that they often confuse God with their religious tradition's

8. Job 11:7–9.

"packaging" of God (say, the religious music tradition), and find "God" boring. But God is anything but boring. He created everything, much of which, like the duck-billed platypus, is delightfully funny. And he is the Source behind all that is beautiful—whether a piece by Mozart or an air move by Michael Jordan, and whether that beauty is fragile like a violet or terrifying like a volcano. C. S. Lewis writes:

> We are half-hearted creatures, fooling about with drink and sex and ambition when infinite joy is offered us, like an ignorant child who wants to go on making mud pies in a slum because he cannot imagine what is meant by the offer of a holiday at the sea. We are far too easily pleased.[9]

No wonder Lewis, in *The Last Battle,* compares the pursuit of God to climbing "farther up and farther in." To be called to know God is to be invited on the greatest adventure imaginable, more dangerous and significant than Frodo's trip to Mordor, more full of surprises than Alice's visit to Wonderland, and more fulfilling than the most satisfying love story you can think of. There will always be more to know and enjoy of him.

Self-discovery (secondary calling), and not just God-discovery (primary calling), takes a lifetime. And this is so for two reasons at least. First of all, we are sinners, which means in part that we are a tangled web of self-rejection and self-vaunting. We resent how we have been wired, and covet the endowments of other people ("if only I were as smart as she, or as good looking as he"), sometimes so tenaciously that it takes decades (and untold miseries) for us to let go of

9. C. S. Lewis, *The Weight of Glory* (Grand Rapids: Eerdmans, 1972), 2.

our identity fantasies and begin to receive with gratitude who we actually are.

To self-rejection we add self-deception. That is, we are also astoundingly adept at lying, even to ourselves, about our moral condition, always finding something or someone else to blame for what we have done wrong. Our experience confirms Jeremiah's sobering judgment that "The heart is deceitful above all things and beyond cure. Who can understand it?"[10]

The difficulty we have figuring ourselves out has other, happier, sources. God's design, and not just our waywardness, makes us mysterious. We are "fearfully and wonderfully made,"[11] and the God who "wired" us initially continues his work, molding us through the complexity of life experience. We are God's "poem." Both nature and nurture are in his hands. Dare we believe that this Craftsman's work might be less subtle or marvelous than Michelangelo's? Dare we expect to figure ourselves out by the time we reach college, or at midlife, or even on our death beds? The Caller alone knows my calling in fullness, and I must await the end of my earthly life to receive the "name" that is uniquely mine.[12]

In the meantime, the best course of action, as we shall see, is faithfulness to God's call at every level—the faithful pursuit of God, faithful stewardship, and faithful service. The road to self-discovery and God-discovery is marked not so much by solitude and introspection as by simple decisions, made every

10. Jer. 17:9.

11. Ps. 139:14.

12. The Greek word translated "workmanship" in Eph. 2:10 is "poema." See Gal. 4:9 ("But now that you know God—or rather are known by God . . .") and Rev. 2:17 ("To him who overcomes, I will . . . give him a white stone with a new name written on it, known only to him who receives it").

day, to do what is right. The faithful pilgrim can expect, at the end of his days, to hear the Redeemer say, "Well done, good and *faithful* servant! You have been *faithful* with a few things; I will put you in charge of many things. Come and share your master's happiness."[13]

13. Matt. 25:21.

Questions
for Reflection and Discussion

1. Compare primary, secondary, and tertiary calling.

    - *Think of two or three situations that illustrate how tertiary calling gets in the way of secondary calling. Have you experienced this frustration? If so, how have you coped with it?*

    - *How have you been tempted to allow secondary calling to undermine primary calling?*

2. Have you ever discovered significance and joy in a mundane ("tertiary") task because you realized that it, too, was from God? What happened? How can you cultivate a deeper appreciation of the holiness of all three forms of calling—especially tertiary?

3. How has God "hard-wired" you? What, in other words, do you particularly love to do? What do you have aptitude in?

4. Do a personal calling inventory by answering the following questions:

- *What role do I permit God to play in my work/ studies/child-raising/career search (whatever occupies the bulk of your time at the moment)? Consider not just the relationships at work, but also the work itself—what I do, why I do it, how I do it. Try to be specific in your answer.*

- *What effect is my pursuit of career and success having on the relationships in my life? How would a close friend or family member answer this question? (If you don't know, ask.)*

- *Read Philippians 3:4b-13: Can I honestly say with Paul that what I want most in life is to know and enjoy God? What choices in my use of time, gifts, and money show this priority?*

- *Am I impatient with God because he is not making clear precisely and quickly just what I am supposed to be doing with life? If so, why? How can this waiting period be used to cultivate primary calling?*

- *Do I bring God to life and work with me? Do I bring him to the library? Do I look to him to be my teacher as I do math and my boss as I work a deal? Do I enjoy and share with him the things I am discovering about myself and about life as I work in his presence?*

2

Creation
A Quest with a Built-in Purpose

I am fearfully and wonderfully made.

Psalm 139:14

3

God's Workmanship

heard somewhere of a particularly brutal form of Nazi torture. Guards would at times order concentration camp inmates to dig a huge hole in the ground and transfer the excavated dirt to a far section of the compound. After dumping the soil in the remote area, the prisoners would then be required to carry the dirt back to the original location and refill the hole. Immediately upon coming full cycle, they would then be told to repeat what they had just done, again and again. They began to take their own lives. Certainly the sheer exhaustion played a role in their despair; but what really got to them was the pointlessness of the exercise.

I remember experiencing my own, much milder, version of the same trauma. Sometime during my early teens, as I was blissfully enjoying the warmth and euphoria that customarily attend early spring, a disturbing thought entered my mind: *Your present state of mind, Charlie, is nothing more than the emotional upturn that you experienced at the same time last year and that you will experience at the same time next year. It is no more than part of a cycle that will continue throughout your life until it is broken by your death.*

We find ourselves asking, "What is my life for? Is it just a series of cycles, or is it going somewhere? How do I fit into the scheme of things?" These questions are not narrowly religious questions. They are human questions, and they bother us whatever our background happens to be.

I am happy to report that my troubling reflections that spring afternoon did not lead me to despair. They led me eventually to the transforming discovery that my life really does have a purpose—which is to glorify and enjoy God through his Messiah Jesus. But that discovery, while removing despair from the foundation of my life, did not answer every question about what it would mean, in practical terms, for *me* to glorify and enjoy God in the life that was beginning to unfold before me.

A Road Map, Not a Formula

Most of us try to answer the practical calling question by keeping busy. We operate, wisely, on the principle that you can steer a ship only when it is moving through the water. In other words, we figure that the best way to discover what our lives are for (in the practical sense) is by living our lives for something (or someone) and seeing what happens. We do this instinctively, whether or not we are conscious of it.

We live for the approval of our parents, or for the approval of our peers. We live for the love of another, or for our children. Or we may live for achievement and recognition—first academically and then in a career that we deem (or our society deems) respectable. Or we may live for God, pursuing a full-time calling in ministry. Some live to satisfy a deep personal drive that may have little to do with recognized success—say, to compose music that deeply satisfies. Some live for sports. Some of us live for a cause. Some live for personal peace—to feel good about themselves and get along with everyone.

Such life drives, providing that they do not turn idolatrous (we will discuss this later), can put us on paths that are very useful for self-discovery. The difficulty is that we rarely live for one thing only, even when we are most deeply committed to following God, and the multiple drives often put us on opposing paths.

A young man may find himself, for example, deeply drawn to a career in music, but his parents earnestly desire him to pursue medicine. Another may be a great athlete and a great student, finding himself torn between a career in professional football and a career in business or teaching. A woman may find herself deeply drawn to Bible translation work in Papua New Guinea while at the same time deeply in love with a man who, for health reasons, cannot safely live in that part of the world. Or a couple may feel called to live in the inner city but find that they cannot in good conscience take their children there.

How do we sort these matters out?

49

Getting at the practical answer, as we have been seeing, takes a lifetime and defies formulas. It is not simply a matter of getting some expert to administer a personality inventory test to us and acting on the results. Nevertheless there is a way of thinking about calling that provides us with a helpful road map for the journey. It is an unusual map: it does not provide us with detailed directions, and yet it gives us hope by guaranteeing that we will make it home. It also is pretty explicit about the terrain so as to keep our expectations realistic as we make our way.

The road map in question is a "theology map"—that is, a set of great biblical ideas which, when held together in our minds, take us where we need to go in a healthy way. We will focus on four—Creation, Fall, Redemption in Christ, and Consummation—devoting the rest of this section to the first.

Creation and Calling

Here is an elaboration of the idea of Creation as applied to the question of calling:

> God made me in his image—which means that my life and my work have built-in purpose. God made me in particular—which means that there is a uniqueness about me that he wants me to discover and joyfully to express. God made me to reflect and honor him—which means that I will find myself only as I make his reputation and glory more important than my own. God made me to enjoy him, and for this reason I will discover who I am only as I learn to love him and people (for they too are made in his image and we love him by loving them).

In this chapter and the following four we will unpack this summary under five headings: (1) I matter, (2) my lifework is intrinsically valuable, (3) my lifework is sacred, (4) my lifework is for God's glory, and (5) I'll never discover my calling alone.

I Matter

Somewhere on an urban ghetto wall in the 1960s someone scrawled: "God made me. And God don't make no trash!"

Early in my pastoral career, when I was an associate minister, I received a visitor in my office. He was something of a big shot in our denomination and he had stopped by in hopes of seeing my boss. It was plain throughout our conversation that he was very disappointed to have missed my superior and not at all interested in meeting me. It hurt—it was in fact infuriating—to be slighted in this way.

I have been marginalized from time to time by particular individuals. (Try mentioning at a country club cocktail party that you are a Christian minister and see how quickly whoever it is you are talking with manages to disengage!) I have had it easy compared with many. Others are marginalized constantly by their parents, or by people of a different race, or by a society whose values they cannot satisfy. Still others are marginalized by standards they have imposed on themselves—usually performance standards, sometimes ethical ones.

God never marginalizes us. The next time you despair over your insignificance, spend some time in Psalm 139. It is a rhapsody in three stanzas on God's loving preoccupation with us. The first stanza (vv. 1–6) celebrates his tender and penetrating knowledge of us ("you have searched me and you know me. . . . Before a word is on my tongue you know it completely"), the second (vv. 7–12) wonders over his inescapable presence with us ("If I rise on the wings of the dawn, if I settle on the far side of the sea, even there your hand will guide me, your right hand will hold me fast"), and the third (vv. 13–18) celebrates his creation of us:[1]

> For you created my inmost being; you knit me together in my mother's womb. I praise you because I am fearfully and wonderfully made; your works are wonderful, I know that full well. My frame was not hidden from you when I was made in the secret place. When I was woven together in the depths of the earth, your eyes saw my unformed body. All the days ordained for me were written in your book before one of them came to be.

David writes here not about human beings in the abstract, but about himself ("you knit *me* together"). In so doing he invites us to think about ourselves similarly. God thought about me—about all the days of my life, about the particulars of my personality ("my inmost being") and physiology ("my unformed body"), while I was still in the womb. I am at least as important to God as the Mona Lisa was to Leonardo da Vinci—a great work of art arising from his creative genius.

There Is No One Quite Like Me

I am also unique. No two Rembrandts are precisely the same. They will have much in common, coming as they do

---

1. The remainder of the psalm includes a furious outburst at anyone who would think poorly of such a great God (vv. 19–22) and concludes with a prayer (vv. 23–24).

from the same source, but they will each be distinct. We should expect, then, that though we have much in common with one another, we will each be different, even if we come from the same family and culture.

It is fashionable, particularly in western culture, to over-state each individual's uniqueness. We can use the notion to excuse thoughtless and irresponsible behavior or to invite a selfish and harmful indulgence in personal fulfillment. I have a friend whose teenage son used to try, unsuccessfully, to get out of family dish duty by saying, "I'm more of an individual—I prefer to do something on my own." The fact is that we have much in common with one another, and (as we shall see) we discover ourselves in community. Nevertheless, we should not be surprised to discover that the God who gave such versatility to the Beatles is himself extremely versatile in his design of people.

What this means, in practical terms, is that we will never discover who we are by permitting ourselves to be crammed into an arbitrary and limiting definition of what it means to be human. ("You are what you earn"; "You are what you do"; "You are what your parents say you are or want you to be"; "You are what your friends/boyfriend/girlfriend say you are.") God is too creative to make any two of us precisely the same. We are right when we find ourselves chafing at the plans that other people often have for us.

Made in God's Image

If I matter simply because I am God's creature (and I do), how much more significant must I be because I am made in God's image. No other creatures—not even the angels in heaven—are described in such terms. Precisely what the words mean is a subject of some discussion. But one thing is very clear: to be made in God's likeness is to possess a very great dignity—a dignity that surpasses that of anything else in creation, for God is the Lord over all creation.

And this great dignity is intrinsic. That is, it precedes my appearance on the scene—or, to be a bit more precise, it accompanies my appearance on the scene. God did not set Adam in the garden, put him to work for a time, and *then* declare him worthy to be called by God's name: He was the image of God before he lifted a finger, and even after he fell into sin.[2] Our immeasurable dignity is ours not because we know we possess it. Nor is it ours because we live up to its meaning. It does not depend on anything that anyone says about us—our parents, our bosses, our friends and enemies, our children, our teachers, our government. It does not even depend on what we may happen to feel about ourselves, or what we may have discovered about ourselves.

We matter, in other words, even when we are completely clueless as to what we have been placed on this earth to do. And this is so because our value is determined solely and absolutely by what God has said and done with reference to us: "Let us make man in our image" (Gen. 1:26).

2. See James 3:9, where fallen human beings are said to be "in God's likeness."

Questions
for Reflection and Discussion

1. Read over the elaboration of the biblical idea of creation (the boxed section of the chapter).

   - *What aspects of this summary are new to you?*
   - *Which do you find most comforting and helpful? Why?*
   - *Which do you find challenging? Why?*
   - *Which do you find hard to understand or believe? Why?*

2. Read Psalm 139 and answer the following questions:

   - *Verses 1–18 can be easily subdivided into three "stanzas," each one six verses long. Distinguish the themes of each stanza.*
   - *What is the tone of verses 1–18? (If you were to set it to music, what would the music sound like?) Why is this the tone?*
   - *Why is the tone in verses 19–22 so different, and how does it make sense, given the content of verses 1–18?*
   - *What comfort and help does Psalm 139 give to you as you struggle to find your place in the scheme of things?*

3. What makes it difficult for people to believe that they are significant? What makes it difficult for you?

When I consider your heavens, the work of your fingers, the moon and the stars, which you have set in place, what is man that you are mindful of him, the son of man that you care for him? You made him a little lower than the heavenly beings and crowned him with glory and honor. You made him ruler over the works of your hands; you put everything under his feet.

Psalm 8:3–6

4

Work Matters

Someone has wisely said: "I don't work to eat; I eat to work." In other words, I am not like Chloe, our (now deceased) pet Labrador, who was perfectly content if she had food in her bowl. Though I need food to keep going, I am not wired simply to eat. I must have work to do—steady, creative activity in my life.

Twice now in my twenty-five years of work as a minister I have enjoyed sabbaticals. I found one of them pretty scary at the outset. I welcomed the rest from customary responsibilities, but I feared four months of rest without direction. I needed work—a different kind of work at a different pace perhaps, but still work. God agrees. Not even ancient Israel's Sabbaths, as strict as they were, were idle; they contained worship, celebration (including eating and singing), and care for the needy.

Work, Career, and Lifework

By work I do not mean simply, or even primarily, career. Nor do I mean something for which we get paid. Nor do I mean a *magnum opus*—that one great contribution to the world we dream of making. I mean something much broader than any of these—what we will call *lifework*. By lifework I mean the entire business of living out my existence in the presence of God.

A substantial part of lifework will for many of us be employment, since we give many hours of our lives to our jobs and careers. It may involve for a tiny fraction of us a singular contribution to our world—such as the Eiffel Tower, or *Les Miserables*, or the Salk vaccine, or the first moonwalk. But Victor Hugo's lifework involved infinitely more than the celebrated novel for which he is remembered. It includes the whole man's engagement with the fullness of the life that God had set before him—large things and small things, social things and intellectual things, noted things and ignored things.

We all need lifework—engagement with the "stuff" of creation. When God commanded the first man and woman to "subdue the earth,"[1] he used agricultural terms to describe and to give value to this need. The Cultural Mandate (what we have come to call this command) teaches us to view all legitimate work as an expression of our essential humanity—our God-likeness. And this is why unemployment is such a terrible thing.

1. Gen. 1:28.

It is not simply that we need money to eat; it is that we were built to work. Though a paycheck should not be the thing that legitimizes work (many—usually women—work long hours rearing children without pay), it often seems to do so. When the money stops, the work stops. And when the working stops, we shrivel up inside. We cease to live according to design and we lose touch with ourselves and with God.

Noble and Creative Work

According to Psalm 8:3–6, work is a royal activity. It reflects the weighty and honorable crown that God has placed on our heads—a crown like God's own crown, since he himself worked when he made us and our world:

> When I consider your heavens, the work of your fingers, the moon and the stars, which you have set in place, what is man that you are mindful of him, the son of man that you care for him? You made him a little lower than the heavenly beings and crowned him with glory and honor. You made him ruler over the works of your hands; you put everything under his feet.

Notice the picture of work that this psalm gives us. It is a richer picture than we get from our word *employment*: it is more like workmanship. God didn't just "go to work" for six days; he crafted the moon and the stars with his fingers. As God put form to the chaotic void, so I am to put form to the chaos with which time and circumstance confront me—ordering time as I plan my summer vacation, and resources compose a letter to my senator or a paper for a course, learn to drive or spell or program, mediate a conflict between friends, run a pass pattern. All such activity is highly valued "image of God" stuff. It is part of how I show forth the God who made me like himself.

Royalty at the Keyboard and on the Field

Think, by way of illustration, of the God-like workmanship in music. In Genesis 1 God takes the material of creation, in all of its chaotic diversity, and divides it out, thus putting order and beauty to it. He divides water from earth, light from darkness, and so forth. We do something very similar in music. Composition, for example, chooses one pitch or cluster of pitches out of the vast sea of pitches available. It does the same with tempo, dynamics, and timbre, crafting something beautiful by multiple acts of separation and realignment.

Acquiring skill in music follows the same pattern. It entails separating my mind and body from a wide range of things I might otherwise be thinking and doing so that I can bring order to pitch, time, dynamics, bodily movement, tone, and so forth. (My parents' efforts to see me learn piano in the third grade failed miserably because my mind and body refused to make the separations necessary to learn the instrument—I preferred to be outside, playing baseball.) Performance also follows this pattern, ordering in real time a vast array of disciplines—singing this series of pitches and not that series, moving this part of my body in this direction and not some other part of my body in some other direction—all for the purpose of producing a synthesis that has beauty. All of this is Godlike activity, a wondrous partnering with God in the production and expression of beauty and truth.

It's the same with learning soccer. There are lots of things a five-year-old can do with grass—she can sit on it, she can pull it up, she can throw it in the air. She might even try eating it. But playing soccer requires that she learn to run on it. There are all sorts of directions she can run, but to play soccer she has to learn to run in certain directions and not others—notably toward the opponent's net, and not her own, if she happens to have possession of the ball. There are all sorts of things she can do with a ball—she can kick it, throw it, try to put it in her mouth—but if she is going to learn soccer, she has to learn not to touch it with her hands, she has to learn to keep it within bounds (except for special defensive reasons), she has to know when to keep it and when to share it, and she has to know when to run toward it and when to run away. (Seven-year-olds love to play swarm ball. Wherever the ball is, there they are—all of them—much to the coach's dismay.)

This may sound prosaic. But it isn't. With the eyes of faith we see it as wondrous God-like activity, an activity for which we were designed. It is why our hearts leap when we see a great soccer player handle the ball. It is at least part of why my heart leapt the first time our son scored a goal.

No Justification Required

Because lifework has intrinsic worth, it does not have to produce something tangible or obviously useful to have value. Francis Schaeffer pointed out that God filled the Garden of Eden with "useless beauty"—trees whose only function seems to have been to look good.[2] No doubt there were, in addition, many

2. "And the LORD God made all kinds of trees grow out of the ground—trees that were pleasing to the eye and good for food" (Gen. 2:9).

fruit-bearing trees whose fruit fell untouched and unused by Adam and Eve, a terrible "waste" of resources. Did God waste his time producing those useless trees? I don't think so.

Four Vocation Stories

A young man I know entered college as a math and physics major. Halfway through his freshman year he called his parents to tell them that, though he liked math and physics, he was not Albert Einstein II (like most of his fellow math majors), and he needed to get out. So he switched to pre-med biology, which he completed by the end of his junior year. That summer he studied for and sat for the MCAT exam. His senior year, he took a series of electives that interested him—studio art, choral conducting, music theory, and Hindu mythology. In the spring of that final year he informed his parents that he really was not interested in medicine. He desired instead to be a composer. Following college he worked for four years as a youth minister, discovering as he did so an increasing zeal for Christian ministry while at the same time retaining his interest in music. As I write, he is entering his second year of seminary.

Consider another, better-known story. Vincent Van Gogh, a Dutch minister's son, served as a mission preacher before he gave himself over to the painting that made him so famous after his death.

Here is a third. I know a brilliant woman who holds a Ph.D. in biology and received her B.S. from Harvard, magna cum laude and Phi Beta Kappa. She did her advanced degree in record time while raising a family, and was told that she was one of the most able students her thesis advisor had ever seen. She could have chosen any number of high-powered careers in medicine or science, but chose, because of family obligations, a career as a high school science teacher. At times, she has spoken with frustration about what might have been.

One final story. I know a man with a master's degree in social work who is married to a pediatrician. A number of years ago, when their children were young, he elected to stay home with the children while his wife stayed on at work. Though the decision made sense economically, it was a decision that led to much frustration and loneliness for him, as it often does for stay-at-home mothers.

Wasted Lives?

What are we to make of these lives? Is the first a waste because so much time and energy were expended on things that did not line up with what might well be a life calling in ministry? Was Van Gogh's life a waste because he abandoned the ministry for a career in painting that produced no recognition until after his suicide? Is the science teacher's life a waste because her fine mind—a mind that might have made a significant contribution to public health—has poured out its energies instead on correcting countless lab reports and raising children? Is a professionally trained stay-at-home parent's life a waste because he does not use his training, receives no pay for it, and rarely has anything concrete to show for his efforts at the end of the day?

The God who made lovely trees in a far-off corner of the Garden of Eden—a corner that Adam and Eve may never have managed to visit—says "No!" These lives are not wasted. Legitimate work of all sorts—today's work (whether it pays or not, whether it leads to the same sort of work or some very different sort of work tomorrow)—does count. Certainly the brokenness of our world and our hearts can frustrate and poison our work (we will consider this later), but this does not make the work itself insignificant.

As I sit at my computer, writing and rewriting this paragraph, I am bringing order to words. And even if my revision is weak, even if you disagree strongly with what I am trying to say, even if (horrors!) this book never sells, my efforts at word craft will have mattered; for such efforts reflect the work of the glorious Creator, in whose image I have been made. The next time you find yourself struggling over a project, or frustrated over a failed initiative, or depressed over lack of recognition, remember that the God in whose image you have been made looked upon all that he had created and noted with deep satisfaction that "it was very good."[3]

A Way of Saying Thanks

Lifework, whether or not we get paid for it, can become an obsession (we will discuss this problem later). But when this happens it is not the work's fault; it is our fault. Work is good. And working hard at what I have been given to do, working hard at what I am good at (even when I don't feel like it), is part of how I say, "Thank you," to God. It is a form of worship, part of how I respond to my primary calling (to know and love God) in the midst of my quest to know myself (secondary calling). This is why Paul enjoins slaves as he does:

3. Gen. 1:31.

> Slaves, obey your earthly masters in everything; and do it, not only when their eye is on you and to win their favor, but with sincerity of heart and reverence for the Lord. Whatever you do, work at it with all your heart, as working for the Lord, not for men, since you know that you will receive an inheritance from the Lord as a reward. It is the Lord Christ you are serving.[4]

Though we should not use this text to excuse slavery (now or in the past), we should still use it as a standard for work. We work with "sincerity of heart," even when no one is looking, even when the work is boring, even when we aren't paid for it, even when the work environment is unjust, even when the work yields no easily quantifiable or readily satisfying results. And we do this because the Lord, who himself works, is our boss. He sees us, he values us and our efforts, and he will eventually compensate us, even if no one else does.

When we see the Creator's hand in the gifts and opportunities that have come our way, and when we grasp that his heart is kind and respectful toward us, we will repudiate the attitude of the third steward in the Parable of the Talents. He buried the talent he had been given, asserting that the one who had given it to him was a hard master who reaped where he had not sown. We will, instead, embrace the attitude of the first steward who, upon his master's return, declared, "Master, you entrusted me with five talents. See, I have gained five more!"[5]

4. Col. 3:22–24.
5. See Matt. 25:14–30.

Questions
for Reflection and Discussion

1. Why, according to this chapter, is work so important? Why is unemployment often so devastating to people?

2. Distinguish between career and *lifework*. Why is it important to define work more broadly than career?

3. What threatens your sense of the significance of your lifework? Of your career (if you have one)? What needs to happen before you feel that your lifework is valuable? What needs to happen before you feel that your career is valuable? Why?

4. Ephesians 2:10 reads: "For we are God's workmanship [Greek, *poema,* from which we get "poem"], created in Christ Jesus to do good works, which God prepared in advance for us to do." Spend some time talking to God or a group of friends about how he made you and how you feel about his workmanship. Talk honestly about struggles you have with contentment, about identity confusion, about impatience. Where you are genuinely grateful,

give thanks to God. Where you are bitter, try to analyze why, confess what is wrong, and ask for forgiveness and help.

5. Is your lifework a way of saying, "Thank you," to God? How does your thanksgiving come to expression? If there is no thanksgiving in your lifework, why isn't there?

When I run, I feel God's pleasure.

Eric Liddel, *Chariots of Fire*

And on that day there shall be inscribed on the bells of the horses, "Holy to the LORD." And the pots in the house of the LORD shall be as the bowls before the altar. And every pot in Jerusalem and Judah shall be holy to the LORD of hosts, so that all who sacrifice may come and take of them and boil the meat of the sacrifice in them.

Zechariah 14:20–21 ESV

5

Everything Is Kosher

We have seen that the great idea of creation fills us and our lifework with deep and inherent significance. More than that, as we will see in this chapter, the idea makes all work sacred. The biblical notion of creation, in other words, introduces us to a world in which God shows up everywhere.

As I write this, a good friend of mine is struggling with whether to go to seminary or music school. He loves Christian ministry and he loves choral conducting—and he is good at both of them. An earnest Christian, his question is not, "Is either career OK with God?" Rather, he is asking, "Which of these careers is the better one? Which would please God more?" Assuming that he cannot find a way to combine the two, how would you counsel him, and why?

The answers to such questions are not as clear as we might think. They are clear only if we have been taught to carve up life arbitrarily into "sacred" and "secular." Consider another series of questions. Which is more spiritual: Attending a seminar on personal evangelism or attending a seminar exploring whether or not global warming is a problem? Attending a prayer meeting or attending a town meeting on affordable housing in your neighborhood? Being a missionary or being a banker? If you have quick answers to any of these questions, then you do not understand the meaning of the doctrine of creation very well, for the doctrine of creation makes all legitimate work sacred.

Which Career?

This means, for one thing, that no particular calling is inherently more spiritual than another. "Full-time Christian service" is a misleading term. Every believer is (or should be) a full-time believer and therefore in full-time Christian service. Jesus said, "If *anyone* would come after me, he must deny himself and take up his cross and follow me."[1] Being a campus staff worker or a pastor is not inherently

1. Mark 8:34.

more holy or pleasing to God than being a banker or a police officer.

What makes my choice to pursue a particular career "holy" or "unholy" is not the career itself (unless the career is, say, mafia contract killing or prostitution). It is other things—all of which center around primary calling. For example, I can ask myself, "Am I pleasing God by choosing a career that is more or less consistent with how I am wired? Or am I doing it simply to make money or please my parents, or because it's easy, or because my friends are doing it?" What makes a legitimate activity spiritual is not the activity itself, but whether it is done by faith and in love.[2]

In the classic film *Chariots of Fire*, missionary Eric Liddel and his sister Jenny have a heart-to-heart conversation about his plans to stay in Scotland and compete in the Olympics before returning to the mission field in China. Jenny desperately wants him to return immediately, fearing that the preoccupation with running is spiritually dangerous. But he gently refuses. After some back and forth, Eric says, "Jenny. God made me for China. But he also made me fast. And when I run, I feel God's pleasure."

In this simple formulation Eric says something quite profound about calling. He reminds Jenny that all good gifts are from God and that therefore all good gifts, taken together, constitute the base from which we must seek to discern our calling in life. Preaching in China is not inherently more holy

2. "But the man who has doubts is condemned if he eats, because his eating is not from faith; and everything that does not come from faith is sin" (Rom. 14:23). "If I give all I possess to the poor and surrender my body to the flames, but have not love, I gain nothing" (1 Cor. 13:3).

or sacred than running in Paris. His statement does not, of course, provide an easy formula for decision-making when God's good gifts seem to be at odds with each other. Liddel must make a hard decision—in this case to arrange the conflicting callings along a time line: Paris first, then China. But he does this freely before God, his sister, and the Missionary Society. He properly understands that, since God counts all legitimate work as holy, so can he.

Which Music?

Consider music. Is it more holy to compose hymns for worship or hip-hop for general consumption? Is Bach more suitable for public worship than Coltrane? Is "Amazing Grace" sung off-key by a sincere believer better suited for church than a Chopin mazurka performed brilliantly by an inquiring unbeliever who happens to be the friend of the choir director? Is a congregation's spontaneous rendering of "Great Is Thy Faithfulness" more spiritual than a magnificent performance of Mozart's Requiem in Lincoln Center? Is it a higher thing to be a choir director than a jazz drummer or a concert violinist?

If our answer to any of these questions comes too quickly, we may have permitted a sacred/secular split to infiltrate our thinking. No particular sequence of tones or progressions, no particular rhythmic pattern (that is, no particular musical style) is inherently more sacred than any other. Some styles may carry with them unhelpful associations for certain people, or may be too unusual to be introduced into certain worship contexts, or may seem not to fit the lyrics very well

(I say "seem" because our sense of what fits depends in large measure on our particular experience of music in worship, not on God-given absolutes that we can easily identify). Love will bear such considerations in mind in the selection of music for worship; but love will not elevate one style over another in any absolute sense.

As for the choice between "Amazing Grace" and Chopin: certainly, God looks for hearts to praise him—but this does not mean that he is indifferent to off-key singing. The One who made beautiful trees in the Garden of Eden will not in the end have to choose between beautiful attitudes and beautiful sounds, and we risk dividing his world when we too readily choose "Amazing Grace" sung flat by the Christian over the Chopin played well by a seeker. Of course, we also risk dividing God's world if, as a matter of policy, we maintain that only "professionals" may offer worship in public services (much will depend, if we are processing the issue properly, on the mission of the church in its particular setting—not on a sacred/secular division in our thinking).

Consider the choice between hymns at church and Mozart at Lincoln Center, or the choice between a jazz gig and a choir job. We ought to be able to worship in either setting, since "every good and perfect gift comes from above."[3] This is not to make the concert hall a substitute for gathering intentionally with God's people to adore him. It is simply to say that all beauty is from God, and he can therefore be found (and intends to be found) wherever we encounter beauty. No wonder that J. S. Bach, the patron saint of legitimate church music

3. James 1:17.

for many people, wrote, "To the Glory of God," on all sorts of composition, both "sacred" and "secular."

Too Close for Comfort?

This notion—that the doctrine of creation makes everything sacred—is exciting. But it can also be disturbing. Religious people often do not like it. It can make it too difficult to figure out whether some person or activity is "OK." We are often less comfortable with the real God than with our more manageable tailor-made versions of him.

Non-religious people are often disturbed as well, but for a different reason. I have friends who are intrigued by the "God thing," but are nervous about it getting out of hand. They are open to spirituality and want somehow to find satisfaction in that part of their lives. But they want to be free to arrange the other aspects of life (career, relationships, studies, lifestyle) on their own. They don't want God "showing up" everywhere.

I understand this fear. It is scary to cast your life fully into the hands of a Person you may barely know and whose very existence you may sometimes doubt. God is much safer in small doses and in limited areas. It can also be embarrassing, especially if your friends find faith to be stupid and irrelevant.

What helps is realizing that all of us, religious and non-religious (including agnostic and atheistic friends), habitually cast our lives into the arms of something. The question is never *whether* I am relying deeply on something to watch over my life; it is always *whom* or *what* am I leaning on? And then there is the follow-up: is that person or thing stable and good enough to bear the weight of my life?

The biblical idea of creation reassures us because it invites us to cast our lifework fully into the Creator's hands, and he alone is consistently good, wise, and trustworthy. People, circumstances, and our own resources are not.

Questions
for Reflection and Discussion

1. How would you counsel my friend whose story appears in the second paragraph of the chapter? Why?

2. Discuss or reflect on the questions in the third paragraph of the chapter. How would you answer them, and why?

3. What is meant by the illegitimate "sacred/secular" divide discussed in this chapter? Why is it illegitimate? How do you see that split working in your own ways of thinking and behavior, or where have you seen it in your own background?

4. Describe Eric Liddel's dilemma. How did he resolve it? On what grounds?

5. Discuss or reflect on the following, found at the end of the chapter. Do you agree or disagree? Why? Where have you tended to cast your life hopes, and what has happened?

What helps is realizing that all of us, religious and non-religious (including agnostic and atheistic friends), habitually cast our lives into the arms of something. The question is never <u>whether</u> I am relying deeply on something to watch over my life; it is always <u>whom</u> or <u>what</u> am I leaning on? And then there is the follow-up: is that person or thing stable and good enough to bear the weight of my life? The biblical idea of creation reassures us because it invites us to cast our lifework fully into the Creator's hands, and he alone is consistently good, wise, and trustworthy. People, circumstances, and our own resources are not.

O magnify the LORD with me, and let us exalt his name together.

Psalm 34:3 KJV

6

Show and Tell

God has made us "in his image." I am a portrait of God—only it is a moving, working portrait. My life, when it is unfolding according to design, is like a film, and viewers of all sorts (angelic and human) get to see God at work. This task of showcasing God is so fundamental to what I have been made for that I will not figure myself out very well unless I make it a priority. I find myself, in other words (and ironically), only as I make "finding myself" less important than finding and showcasing God.

Let me put the matter another way. If I am "the image," then God is "the substance." This does not, of course, mean that I am not real or important. But what it does mean is that my reality and importance derive from him. God the Creator is at the center of things—not I. If I try to put myself at the center I will enter a universe that does not actually exist—a fantasy world. The result is that I will never truly discover myself. I will be like a baby who never grows up because he never learns to live with the reality that his needs are not the only (or even the most important) needs that exist. Or I will be like a husband who barely knows who he is because he never listens to his wife.

An Astronomer Finds God

Harvard astronomy professor Owen Gingerich developed a passion for the stars as a child. But he struggled as a young man over whether to make a career of it. What tipped the scales for him was the advice of a believing professor. Here is a portion of his story:

> For as long as I can remember, I have been fascinated by the stars. My parents said that it all began on a stiflingly hot night in Iowa, when my mother moved cots outside for sleeping—and as a five-year-old I discovered the stars. Later, in a liberal arts college in Indiana, I built my own telescope, but I studied chemistry because that seemed so much more useful for mankind than something as arcane as astronomy. Through a quite unpredictable series of circumstances I had an opportunity to spend a summer at the Harvard Observatory as an assistant to the famous astronomer Harlow Shapley, and this inflamed my enthusiasm for the celestial science. But still

I held back, uneasy about the justification of astronomy as a career choice. At that point my college math professor gave me some advice. "If you really want to be an astronomer," he said, "you really ought to go for it. After all, we shouldn't let the atheists take over any field." So I applied to the Harvard graduate program in astronomy and was accepted.[1]

Professor Gingerich's passion gave him insight into God's call on his life. But what gave him confidence to commit his life professionally to that passion, what has harnessed that passion through the years, and what has kept that passion from degrading over time into mere personal indulgence has been, it seems, a God-honoring purpose. He writes: " 'The heavens declare the glory of God,' says the psalmist, and I believe that is true in many wonderful ways."[2]

The heavens are not, for Professor Gingerich, the platform from which he gets to show off what he knows. They exist on their own and they have a story to tell. His job is humbly to listen and report.

Making God Bigger

In Psalm 34:3 David cries out with joy, "O magnify the LORD with me, and let us exalt his name together." *Magnify* (used here in the King James Version) is a better translation than the more common *glorify*—for the root of the Hebrew word used here is the word we translate "great." David is shouting, "Let's make God great! Let's make him bigger and

---

1. Owen Gingerich, "More Than Machines," in Kelly Monroe, ed., *Finding God at Harvard* (Grand Rapids: Zondervan, 1996), 268.
2. Ibid.

bigger! Let's blow up the three-by-five so that it fills the largest screen in Hollywood!"

How strange this language is when you think about it. Isn't God already big—isn't he already infinite? Indeed he is. The problem lies with us. For multiple reasons we have difficulty seeing his greatness and therefore must train our vision. We also have difficulty giving God center stage and therefore must train our hearts. And we must not only train our vision and hearts, but help other people to train theirs as well.

How do we "magnify" him? We do it by taking note of and shedding light on the wonders of God's workmanship—wonders that are already present but hidden or unacknowledged.

Think for example of the discoveries in physics. Sir Isaac Newton and his early successors unveiled for all to see the astonishing symmetry of and consistency in things. Those who came later (the founders of modern physics) brought to the ironclad beauty of that earlier model a subtlety and mystery that it lacked. Both groups, whether they admitted it or not, were "magnifying" God—the first showing forth his power and the other his mystery.

Is light a wave or is it a particle? Sometimes it acts like a wave, but sometimes it does not. We cannot simply transfer our experience of ripples on a pond to our understanding of light—at least we cannot do it all the time. This mysterious finding is true to the way things are, and it is God's invitation to adore him as the infinite one—the one whose ways are not our ways, the one who does not seek counsel from us.

Godly educators magnify God, opening the eyes of their students to God's handiwork in the nuance, beauty, complexity, and power of creation. We all do it whenever we tell a good story that gives insight into how God has designed things or how he works with people. We all do it when we champion the truth in some way. We do it, as well, whenever we praise God in worship, trust him in adversity, or make decisions, whether large or small, whose purpose is to honor God through obedience to his Word.

Humble Observers

If God is to get bigger, then I must get smaller. Part of what this means is that I need to submit humbly to what he shows me about the way things are. It has been truly said that "all truth is God's truth." Truth is truth even when it is told by someone I do not like, even when it is uncomfortable. Truth is truth even when it overturns a paradigm that I have built my research career upon.

My wife and I had the privilege while in college of meeting Dr. R. Hooykaas, a leading scholar in the history of science and professor of that subject at the University of Utrecht. We learned in our discussions with him that he made a habit of promoting the work of bright young scholars—especially when that work challenged accepted scientific theories. He knew from experience how quickly research can lose its integrity because of vested interest and, for that reason, counted it his obligation as a Christian to keep shaking up existing paradigms.

If the "heavens declare the glory of God" and if "the earth shows forth his handiwork," then we must let them speak, even if we (or others) do not like what they say. Whether we are arguing over the sun or the earth being at the center of the cosmos (an old argument, long since settled) or over the scientific integrity of Intelligent Design, God calls us to humility—not only with each other, but also before the evidence to be found in what he has made. And this is true not only in science, but in every sphere of life.

Worship While You Work

We noted in the previous chapter that all work is sacred. What we are noting now is this: to say that all work is sacred is to say that all work, like everything in life, is for God. Snow White's dwarf companions whistled while they worked. We take it a step higher: we worship while we work.

And our worship is not extraneous to the work. We don't, in other words, simply praise God that the math homework is done, or that we got a good grade in math. We worship in the work itself. We praise God by the diligence with which we undertake it, we praise him by depending on him for the strength to do it, we praise him for the beauty of the math itself, we seek appropriate ways to show colleagues his beauty there, and (as we have opportunity) we use the math skills we have acquired for God-honoring purposes. I realize that, in your case, finding beauty in math may be a bit like a drowning man finding beauty in a fresh gulp of seawater. But I am sure you get the idea. Just replace math with whatever your "thing" is.

Our pursuit of calling unfolds in God's world, not ours. To paraphrase St. Paul, our gifts, opportunities, and discoveries all come from God; they all find expression through the life that he gives us; and they all rightly flow back to him, showing forth his beauty, love, truth, and power through us.[3] Our calling, in other words, is "missional"—not in the narrow sense

3. Rom. 11:36.

of going into foreign missions (though it might include this), but in the much broader sense of finding and promoting him in everything we do.

Jesus said that if we seek to find ourselves we will lose ourselves. If, in other words, we make self-discovery the first order of business in our lives, self-discovery will turn out to be the thing that does not happen. Jesus goes on to say, "But whoever loses his life for me will find it."[4] There is a strange irony here—but it makes sense in a world where everything comes from God and exists for God. If I make God's glory and honor "everything," then everything else, including figuring myself out, will fall in line. But if I make my glory and honor everything, I will be looking at things through the wrong end of the telescope. Reality will be distorted and far away. I will miss my true purpose.

4. Matt. 16:24–25.

Questions
for Reflection and Discussion

1. Think about whatever occupies the bulk of your waking hours (it could be school, or childcare, or employment of some sort). Where and how is God revealing himself in that setting? How do, or might, you therefore magnify him in that setting?

2. Discuss the following paraphrase of Jesus' famous saying. Identify at least one way in which you are trying to find yourself in your lifework and one way that you could make that work more God-centered.

   If I try to find myself in my work, I will lose myself; but if I aim to find God in my work, then I will find myself.

3. Discuss Professor Hooykaas's approach to the work of bright young scholars. Why did he consider that approach to be a Christian obligation? How might you do something similar in your area(s) of influence?

4. Discuss the following statement, found toward the end of the chapter. Feel free to shift the subject to something else (such as gardening, or teaching children, or selling real estate, or training for volleyball) if math isn't your thing.

> And our worship is not extraneous to the work. We don't, in other words, simply praise God that the math homework is done, or that we got a good grade in math. We worship in the work itself. We praise God by the diligence with which we undertake it, we praise him by depending on him for the strength to do it, we praise him for the beauty of the math itself, we seek appropriate ways to show colleagues his beauty there, and (as we have opportunity) we use the math skills we have acquired for God-honoring purposes.

So God created man in his own image, in the image of God he created him; male and female he created them.

Genesis 1:27

7

Finding Ourselves in Community

pastor a church near Columbia University on the Upper West Side of Manhattan. As hard-working, independent, and career-tracked as many in my young congregation are, most are more desperate for community than they are for success. Again and again, comments about our church, whether criticisms or compliments, focus on our community life.

Why does community (or the hope of it) draw us so powerfully? In part because we are desperate to find out who we are, and that discovery comes only in the context of relationships. Left alone we lose our bearings—even to the point of psychosis. Tom Hanks's marooned character in *Cast Away*, for example, turns a soccer ball into a friend named Wilson. Denzel Washington's character in *Hurricane* (the prize-fighter "Hurricane Carter," who was falsely convicted of murder and spent many years in prison before he was exonerated) is so desperate for community while in solitary confinement that his personality splits.

Community draws us out. It unveils us.

In the Image of the Trinity

Why is healthy community so necessary for self-discovery? Because we are created in God's image and God is himself community—one God in three Persons.

At an earlier time in my life the mystery of the Trinity struck me as true but irrelevant. It was there in the Bible, but I couldn't see that mystery's connection to me. I feel very different now.[1]

The fact that God is, and has always been, community explains why love is so important to us and to people everywhere. It explains why the story of Romeo and Juliet breaks our hearts, why broken homes devastate children, and why there is rarely, if ever, such a thing as a peaceful divorce. It explains why we spend billions of dollars annually singing, writing about, and listening to accounts of love found and love lost. It explains why Woody Allen confesses that all his films

1. A profound treatment of the meaning of the Trinity is found throughout the pages of Miroslav Wolf's remarkable book, *Exclusion and Embrace* (Nashville: Abingdon Press, 1996).

"deal with the greatest of all difficulties—love relationships. Everybody encounters that. People are either in love, about to fall in love, on the way out of love, looking for love or a way to avoid it."[2]

Let me press the point. Being made "in the image of God" involves more than possessing the traits we ordinarily associate with our activities as individuals—creativity, choice, self-consciousness, and so on. It includes a social dimension as well. Male and female, together, are not "images of God," but "the image of God."[3] In an unfallen Paradise (where Adam enjoyed open communion with God and fear-free dominion over the animals) God nevertheless said, "It is not good for the man to be alone."[4] Adam's naming of the animals only serves to emphasize his loneliness and paves the way for the first human friendship, when at last God brings to the man someone who is like him. He does not discover himself until Eve appears.[5]

2. Graham McCann, *Woody Allen, New Yorker* (Cambridge, Polity: 1990), 22. Quoted by John Stott, *Why I Am a Christian* (Downers Grove, IL: InterVarsity, 2003), 109.

3. Gen. 1:27.

4. This phrase in Gen. 2 jars us, given the constant refrain in Gen. 1, "and God saw that it was good."

5. Commenting on this scene, Henri Blocher writes, "Scripture could not underline better the degree to which solitude contradicts the calling of humanity." (*In the Beginning* [Downers Grove, IL: InterVarsity, 1984], 96). Derek Kidner seconds him: "Man will not live until he loves, giving himself away (vs. 24) to another on his own level." (*Genesis: An Introduction and Commentary*, [Downers Grove, IL: InterVarsity Press, 1977], 65). Blocher further points out that Adam's first use of the personal pronoun occurs only after Eve is brought to him: "This at last is bone of *my* bone and flesh of *my* flesh." (Blocher, *In the Beginning*, 96).

Finding Ourselves at Church?

We all, and not simply Adam, need friendship for self-discovery. And we need more than one friend. I count my wife of more than thirty years to be my best friend, but she cannot possibly bring out all that I am, nor can I possibly bring out all that she is. We both need additional friends if we are going to discover and express the range of gifts God has planted within us. C. S. Lewis writes:

> In each of my friends there is something that only some other friend can fully bring out. By myself I am not large enough to call the whole man into activity; I want other lights than my own to show all his facets. Now that Charles is dead, I shall never again see Ronald's reaction to a specifically Caroline joke. Far from having more of Ronald, having him "to myself" now that Charles is away, I have less of Ronald.[6]

Where do we find these other friends? The best place is the church.

I say this fully aware of how inhibiting the church can be. A teenager I know was playing jazz one Sunday evening on the piano in the church basement. A woman in the congregation, a leader in the music ministry, abruptly stopped him by closing the keyboard cover on his hands. Though she did not hurt him physically (her act was firm but not violent), she wounded his spirit. Worse, she vividly promoted a lie in God's name. She said, in effect, "This thing that you are doing—this musical style, this form of beauty—displeases God. If you continue in

6. C. S. Lewis, *The Four Loves* (New York: Harcourt, Brace and Company, 1960), 92.

it, you will have to do so somewhere else, in some less holy place."

This sort of thing frequently happens in churches, and it is one of the reasons that so many of us run away from church. The irony is that God means the church to be the best and safest place to discover and be yourself. It is the environment where my gifts are "for the common good," the place where self-giving love triumphs in the safety of the heavenly Father's love.[7] It is God's "sneak preview" on the heavenly society that the Messiah died to create:

> I saw the Holy City, the new Jerusalem, coming down out of heaven from God, prepared as a bride beautifully dressed for her husband. And I heard a loud voice from the throne saying, "Now the dwelling of God is with men, and he will live with them. . . . He will wipe every tear from their eyes. . . . " He who was seated on the throne said, "I am making everything new!"[8]

There is no suggestion of inhibition in this picture. God's bride is holy, to be sure, but her holiness is not at odds with her beauty and joy. She is the centerpiece in her Groom's remaking of everything, in which goodness, creativity, rejoicing, and loveliness all combine in one great symphony. By God's design, in other words, the church is the safest and most satisfying environment in which to figure ourselves out. This will certainly be the case when history as we know it comes to

7. 1 Cor. 12:7. See Eph. 5:1: "Be imitators of God, therefore, as dearly loved children, and live a life of love."
8. Rev. 21:2–5.

an end. But we should be working toward it now, for Christ is already in us, "the hope of glory."[9]

A Church Consumer

Here are some thoughts on what we can do. First, we need to stop being church consumers. New York, where my church is located, is full of great churches—meeting at different times and offering a range of musical styles, worship formats, programs, preaching styles, and emphases. It is tempting in such a place to church hop. Some people attend a different church every week, depending on which service time is more convenient on any given Sunday.

New York is not the only place where this problem exists. People all over the country shop for churches that "work for them."

This attitude is terribly wrong. "Church" is not an event. It is people—people whom God calls us to love. What is more, it is in a very important sense an involuntary community of people: we don't choose our brothers and sisters—God does. And sometimes (oftentimes) those people are not terribly compatible with us—not the people we would choose to hang out with. But it is this very incompatibility that is so important, for at least two reasons. First, learning to love the people I don't like is by far the best way to learn how to love (it's easy to love people I happen to like). Second, the church is supposed to be a sociological miracle—a demonstration that Jesus has died and risen to create a new humanity composed of all sorts of people.

Not only is the consumer mindset wrong. It also sabotages self-discovery. For I will find myself only as I learn to listen to

9. Col. 1:27.

others and to give myself away in love to others—even (and perhaps especially) those who are not like me.

"Geoffrey" is a young man in my church whose story appears in the appendix. Here is part of what he says about being a consumer:

> It might seem strange to include not joining a church among a list of rotten things that we do, but it is. It's a really rude thing that we do to God. What were my reasons? First, I was just too busy to get baptized. I just procrastinated on it. Second, why join a church as a member? Two years ago, I started coming to Emmanuel. I took the membership class to deepen my knowledge about the Christian faith and theology, but never signed aboard as a member. I couldn't really do it. Why would I want some other people telling me how to live my life? Why would I want to do that? First, hey, it's between me and Jesus. Church is not filled with perfect angelic people. (I mean, *I'm* here, right?) Why do I want to be accountable or follow guidance from imperfect people?

> But about six months ago, something started to dawn on me. I had turned into a church consumer. Show up, listen to the sermon, maybe stay afterward for coffee hour to say hi to people. It was about me, me, me. What religious warm fuzzies could I get from church? What sort of fun goody bag of intellectual ideas could I take away from the service? I was just a consumer—might as well be at a mall shopping. Is this how Christ, my Savior, Lord, and Friend would want me to relate to his church? Probably not. I started to realize that I have to trust God in all facets of my life. Not getting baptized or joining a church was an act of rebellion against him.

Working for a Better Church

Rather than abandoning the church because it is judgmental or irrelevant, we should work to make the church a place where it is safe to be honest about problems. The best place to begin is with personal vulnerability.[10] Alcoholics Anonymous has proven to be so effective because mutual honesty makes everyone feel safe with one another. We will find it very difficult to discover God's calling if we are trapped in perfectionism, food addiction, sexual sin, or even a guilt complex. And we will find it very difficult to escape those traps if there is no safe community that will help us make the escape. The church is perfectly equipped to be that community because it is made up of a people all of whom admit that they need help and all of whom celebrate a Savior who died to heal them.

Rather than abandoning the church because it resists creativity, we should work patiently to build a church culture that is open to new things. Our church occasionally commissions new pieces of music—even "risky" pieces that are unfamiliar and don't sound very "holy" to the average churchgoer. Our reasoning is simply this: Why should the concert hall get all the new stuff when the church is the place where God is "making all things new"?

Rather than despising the church because it has no zeal for doing things well, we should give to the church our very best and make room in the church's mentality for excellence in all that we do. There is often a reverse snobbism in the church. We find it when we hear someone say about

10. "Confess your sins to each other, and pray for each other, so that you may be healed" (James 5:16).

an offertory, "I didn't like it—it was too much of a performance." Such a response suggests that the critic knows the
heart of the person who gave the offertory. It also drives a
wedge between spirituality and hard work, suggesting that
if someone gives his or her very best to an offertory, and
that very best happens to be of a very high caliber (because
that person is very talented), then that offering is somehow
suspect. God put his very best into creation, and his very
best was astonishingly good ("and God saw all that he had
made and, behold, it was very good"); we would never fault
him for being "too professional." So why should we fault
each other?

Rather than despising the church because it makes no
room for those with lesser gifts, we should patiently look for
ways to give appropriate expression to those gifts. One of
the churches I served had a "come-one-come-all" orchestra.
Led by a director who offered free lessons throughout the
year to children of the congregation and their friends, the
orchestra put on two concerts annually. The ensemble for
those concerts was routinely made up of professional musicians, children who had only just begun to play, and people
of every skill level in between. The effect was hardly professional musically but very rich interpersonally. Most important,
it helped create a culture in the church that said, "It's OK
to try things out." And it is in such a culture that people will
find their gifts.

Finding Ourselves Together

We do not need to be married to discover and live out
our calling. The apostle Paul was single—as was Jesus. But

we do need company. And we especially need the church. The simple fact of the matter is that we draw each other out. Our gifts are not for hoarding. If we do not have occasion to share them with people, they remain dormant, and we never discover what they are.

So don't withdraw from people.

Ironically, the best way to find out who you are is not to spend too much time trying to find out who you are. Love people, engage people, and show God to people, and self-discovery will sneak in the back door. As Jesus put it, "Whoever wants to save his life will lose it, but whoever loses his life for me will find it."[11]

---

11. Matt. 16:25.

Questions
for Reflection and Discussion

1. How does the Trinitarian nature of God help us understand our longing for community?

2. Recall an experience in which someone's (perhaps your) decision to get involved with people led to self-understanding.

3. Think about your church experience. How has the church stood in the way of your self-discovery? How has the church helped? What have you done to make the church a place where self-discovery and honesty about personal struggle can flourish? What have you done to inhibit those things?

4. Are you a church consumer? What evidence is there that you are not a consumer when it comes to the actual choices you have made about church involvement over the past year?

5. Read over the section titled "Working for a Better Church." Discuss and reflect on ways you can implement the suggestions.

6. The Bible tells us to care for the spiritual nurture of our children and even ourselves. How do you balance those commands with the equally important command to function as part of the body (not to be a consumer) when it comes to church?

3

The Fall

Something Wrong with Every Step

Cursed is the ground because of you; through painful toil you will eat of it all the days of your life. It will produce thorns and thistles for you, and you will eat the plants of the field. By the sweat of your brow you will eat your food until you return to the ground, since from it you were taken; for dust you are and to dust you will return.

Genesis 3:17–19

8

Thwarted Design

ohn Nash is a mathematical genius and a Nobel Laureate. He is also a man who "walked into the common room [at MIT] one winter morning in 1959 carrying *The New York Times* and remarked, to no one in particular, that the story in the upper left-hand corner of the front page contained an encrypted message from inhabitants of another galaxy that only he could decipher."[1] That episode marked the beginning of a decline into debilitating madness

1. Sylvia Nasar, *A Beautiful Mind* (New York: Simon and Schuster, 1998), 16.

that lasted for thirty years. By all accounts his recovery later in life was a rarity.[2]

The doctrine of creation fills us with enthusiasm and hope as we set out to find our place in the scheme of things. And then we bump into "real life." In the real world brilliant mathematicians unhinge and lose decades of productive life. In the real world parents sometimes pressure children with great artistic ability to pursue medicine. In the real world, our ambition to be the best poisons our enjoyment of what we are doing, fills us with envy, and leads to terrible loneliness.

What's wrong? We are fallen creatures living in a fallen world. In other words, the great idea of Creation we discussed in chapters 3 through 7 does not stand alone. Another big idea—the sad reality of the Fall—must be considered with it. If I grasp the meaning of Creation without grasping the meaning of the Fall, my energy and hope at the outset of any new endeavor, whether it is child rearing or research or learning to drive or learning to play tennis, will give way to disappointment and even bitterness as that endeavor unfolds.

We can summarize the Fall's origin and substance with the following words:

> The human race, represented in our first parents, chose to live apart from God—to seek to become wise without reference to him. As a result God gave them (and us) what they asked for—self-knowledge separated from a safe relationship with the One who made and alone fully understands us. Unsafe with God, we became unsafe with one another. Calling, no

2. "A spontaneous recovery from schizophrenia—still widely regarded as a dementing and degenerative disease—is so rare, particularly after so long and severe a course as Nash experienced, that, when it occurs, psychiatrists routinely question the validity of the original diagnosis." Ibid., 21.

longer a joyous, free, and God-honoring response to our Maker, has become the confused and destructive pursuit of self-gratification. Work, no longer a celebration of our dominion over creation, enjoyed in the presence of the Creator, has become back-breaking and mortal toil.

Notice that the Fall assaults calling from three fronts simultaneously. Nature sabotages calling, we sabotage each other's callings, and we sabotage our own callings. This threefold hostility is relentless and intertwined.

By the Sweat of Our Brows

First, the natural order resists us. At the outset, God gave Adam a lovely and fruitful garden to cultivate: Adam's work came easily. But after the Fall, work became toil. The land grew hard and inhospitable, yielding very little. Tragically, what Adam had been given to subdue ends up subduing Adam: "By the sweat of your brow you will eat your food until you return to the ground, since from it you were taken; for dust you are and to dust you will return."[3]

Frustration and decay afflict our bodies and circumstances, resisting and at times ruining everything we set out to do.[4]

I know a professor who twice lost his PhD dissertation to accidental fire. Since he lived in the era before personal computers and easy photocopying, he had to reproduce and retype his dissertation both times from memory. In the 1950s a very

3. Gen. 3:19.
4. "The creation was subjected to frustration, not by its own choice, but by the will of him who subjected it, in hope that the creation itself will be liberated from its bondage to decay" (Rom. 8:20–21).

talented young dancer, the wife of a famous choreographer, contracted polio, instantly losing all that she had been living and working for. Former President Ronald Reagan, who presided at the fall of Soviet power, spent his final years lingering in a lonely corner of his homestead, a victim of Alzheimer's disease. I remember as a kid being devastated when Sandy Koufax, one of the most astonishing pitchers in major league history, had to retire at age thirty because of arthritis.

Star athletes get the flu just before the big game. Talented young singers get laryngitis on the day of the "must show" audition. Dyslexic children are written off as stupid. A parent has to interrupt his research to raise a Down syndrome child. Drought wipes out hard-working farmers. Earthquakes in Iran, mudslides in Mexico, and tsunamis in Indonesia end lives and livelihoods abruptly, unpredictably, and routinely. Nature, in short, is hostile to our quest for identity and usefulness, a fact of life that the Bible itself acknowledges.

> I have seen something else under the sun:
> The race is not to the swift
> or the battle to the strong,
> nor does food come to the wise
> or wealth to the brilliant
> or favor to the learned;
> but time and chance happen to them all.[5]

Oppressive People and Institutions

Human nature, and not just nature, has fallen. Adam and Eve, formerly safe in their nakedness, suddenly become afraid

5. Eccl. 9:11.

of each other. Vulnerability is now dangerous, so they hide behind makeshift clothes. Adam, who has only recently sung Eve's praise ("This is now bone of my bone and flesh of my flesh"), now attacks her before God ("The woman you put here with me—she gave me some fruit from the tree, and I ate it"). What will follow is a domestic life in which love has given way to oppression and struggle: "Your desire will be for your husband, and he will rule over you."[6] Adam will oppress Eve, and Eve will either desire his protection so inordinately that she will put up with anything or she will seek to usurp his authority in whatever way she can.[7]

We share Adam and Eve's problems. Oppression and struggle (both individual and institutional) routinely infiltrate our experience and sabotage the pursuit of calling. Many a child lacks the confidence to launch out in new ways because of the barrage of put-downs she endures at home. Many great scholars and musicians died at Auschwitz before they were able to publish or compose. Many a black poet in America's antebellum South never got to write poetry because she was too busy tending to her mistress or working the cotton fields. Many a brilliant immigrant to the United States has spent (and spends) a lifetime working long hours at menial tasks simply to make ends meet. Most people throughout human history have had to work long hours at jobs that have provided little or no opportunity to develop their God-given gifts.

6. Gen. 2:23; 3:12, 16.
7. "Your desire shall be" is parallel to "sin . . . desires to have you" (Gen. 4:7) and most likely means that Eve, understandably fearful of Adam's domination, will now seek to usurp his authority in whatever way she can.

Are We Really Entitled?

Once during a visit to Bangladesh I met a young national who was so talented that his government had awarded him, despite his Christian faith, a stipend to attend medical school. Rather than use the stipend for his own advancement, he gave it to the struggling Bangladeshi church. I was astonished, even scandalized, by his sacrifice. I was also shocked by the realization that he was the only one among hundreds of young people I met on that trip who had any hope at all of breaking out of the social and economic constraints of his culture.

I thought of the sense of entitlement that tended to permeate my own mindset ("Of course I ought to be able to get any job I want as long as I work hard for it!") and realized how utterly strange this mindset would be for most of the world. Why should I expect that my academic pursuits, training, and unfolding career would satisfyingly fit my gift mix and avocations when very few people through the ages (including fellow believers) have ever experienced such a happy confluence? The reality of the Fall means that I may have to settle for less than the perfect career (whatever that is).

Po Bronson describes a conference at which he was invited to address more than a hundred CEOs from some of the biggest companies in the United States. They had gathered to dream about ways of stimulating economic growth over the next twenty years—a significant challenge given demographic projections. In answer to the question, "What do employees want?" Mr. Bronson said:

> They want to find work they are passionate about. Offering benefits and incentives are mere compromises. Educating people is important but not enough. We need to encourage

people to find their sweet spot. Productivity explodes when people love what they do.[8]

This observation is true, but not very useful outside the United States. We can afford to make the workplace "sweet" for our employees. Afghanistan, China, and Mexico often cannot.

Problems at School

Not even the industrialized West, for all the remarkable kindness that God has shown to it, escapes the impact of human oppression on calling. Schools are often very dark places. By the design of the Creator they should be places where we discover ourselves and God in a community that works together. Instead they are often oppressive, marked by unhealthy competition, toil, and fear. They tend to crush us into a mold or make us wary survivors. Schools often breed angry loners, some of whom, like the student at Virginia Tech, channel their bitterness ruthlessly.

A friend of mine began her teaching career in one of New York City's marginal schools. Her love and idealism were overwhelmed by what she found: an adversarial local administration, classroom discipline problems so severe that learning was utterly impossible and she was at times in physical danger, hardly any books and supplies, and absolutely no incentives for the rare child who expressed an interest in learning. She left in despair after a year.

8. Po Bronson, *What Should I Do with My Life?* (New York: Random House, 2003), 386.

Higher education has its own forms of oppression. I have a friend at a prestigious music school in New York City. She is a talented cellist who loves her craft and whose skills have garnered high praise. She is also lonely—isolated by the fierce and often malicious competition that fills the culture where she learns her craft. The administration publicly ranks every musician (at last count she was number three out of forty-five). Because of the ranking system, she must constantly watch her back. Once, when she missed an entrance during an orchestra concert, her entire section (all ranked below her and jealous over it) refused to speak with her during the intermission.

Problems at Work

Things do not necessarily get better when schooling is done. Many of us never get work that suits us very well. And those of us who do invariably find elements in our work that are frustrating and demeaning. A small town hardware store may lose business under pressure from Home Depot, meaning shorter hours for its workers, layoffs, or even the end of the business. Unconscious racism or sexism may be imbedded in the design and habits of the work environment. Or it may be deliberate. Or accusations of racism or sexism, even if there is none, may poison the atmosphere and draw us away from the tasks we love and have been given to do. An insecure, micro-managing new boss may make work oppressive. A lazy but well-placed co-worker may make it difficult or even dangerous to put in a good day's work. A bitter employee may make the atmosphere at work toxic.

Most people simply have to take what they can get. Aspiring actors have to wait tables, MBAs have to do temp work,

PhDs have to push mops, textile workers have to work for McDonald's when their factory relocates overseas, hardworking hospital housekeepers have to find new employment when new management calls for new standards they can't meet or new techniques that they can't master. Many cannot find any work at all—or any honest work. So oppressive are the economic and social pressures of their worlds that it is difficult to resist making a living in ways that add to human unhappiness.

Even "reputable" and interesting jobs may confront us with moral ambiguity that we have to wrestle with. Sometimes we may simply have to let go of a really great program or job, where our gifts are being fully used, because the moral compromises entailed in the work we are being asked to do, or in the goals and practices of the department (or company), are more than our consciences can bear.

Should we sell shoes, for example, that are manufactured by children under appalling work conditions? Should we work, consult, or advertise for a company that does this? What do we do if we are in obstetrics and gynecology training as a nurse or physician and are expected to assist in the performance of abortions?

Life and work are full of these sorts of problems. Rarely are human power grabbing and oppression the sole reasons for the problems. But they are nearly always a part of the picture.

Questions
for Reflection and Discussion

1. Read Genesis 3:17–19.

   - *What, according to this text, has happened to work?*

   - *In what particular ways has work become "toil" for you, for people you know, for people in general?*

   - *In what ways does nature itself work against our ability to enjoy God by living out before him all that he has designed us to be? Illustrate from your experience.*

2. Social oppression (from peers, parents, enemies, trends, and institutions) often compromises our ability to live out our callings. Illustrate from your experience, from history, or from current events.

3. Romans 8:20 speaks of creation being "subjected to frustration." What about your present career (whether or not you get paid for it) is frustrating and futile?

4. Do you feel entitled to a life in which your work matches your gifts? Why? Why not?

5. Have you ever been in a job (paid or unpaid) that you really enjoyed, and you discovered that something was very wrong about the goals, practices, or culture of the organization? If so, what did you do about it? If you did not do anything about it, why didn't you?

For although they knew God, they neither glorified him as God nor gave thanks to him, but their thinking became futile and their foolish hearts were darkened. Although they claimed to be wise, they became fools. . . . They exchanged the truth of God for a lie, and worshiped and served created things rather than the Creator—who is forever praised. Amen.

Romans 1:21–22, 25

9

Idolatry
and Self-Sabotage

A terrible flood afflicted parts of Europe in the spring of 2002, submerging a number of priceless paintings in water. The Fall has done to life and work what the overflowing rivers did to those paintings—caking them with mud, warping the canvasses, obscuring the images, ruining the hard work of God-given genius. There is slime and debris everywhere. And the problem is not just with the waters—for we do very little to keep them out. By worshiping our lifework (using it as a God substitute), by despising it (treating it as no more than a means to an end), or by making work oppressive for others, we are constantly punching holes in the dikes.

In other words, the Fall is not just "out there"—in nature and in oppressive people and institutions—as we touched on in chapter 8. The Fall is "in here." We cannot escape the Fall's influence, no matter how promising our circumstances, because we bring our own fallenness with us wherever we go. Consider some of the ways in which we sabotage our own quest for self-discovery.

Idolatry: The Prime Problem

The heart of our problem is idolatry. We take the good things that God generously gives us and turn them into God substitutes. To put it another way, we allow secondary calling (self-discovery) to eclipse primary calling (loving God) and in the process forget the Person who issues both calls. What follows is a portion of "Ying's" story, the fuller version of which appears in the appendix.

> I came to New York City seven years ago at the age of 17 to study classical piano at the Juilliard School of Music. At once, I loved it all and saturated myself with music. I thrust myself into my studies, practicing, learning, going to concerts, and thinking about the nature of the art. For this lonely, searching young girl, music seemed to represent the best of humanity and provide the most meaning and integrity in a cold and empty world. To identify with beauty and truth in music then felt to me a much more tangible and fulfilling spiritual experience than any I had growing up in the church.

So I pursued it with all that I had. It became my religion, my mode of thinking, and my value system.

It was not difficult to find others at Juilliard and in New York City who identified with music in the same way. In a culture where superficiality and senselessness are prevalent, it was not difficult to justify the fervor and enthusiasm with which I and my friends devoted ourselves to the religion of Art.

With this sort of dedication, I met with success and accomplishment during my time at school. The praise I received caused me to build my identity further on music, and I soon made it into an idol that ruled me. All the while, the Lord Jesus, whom I had accepted into my heart at the age of six, waited patiently. Deep down I knew that the faith I had in him was calling me to examine why I was worshiping something else. Like a good "artist/intellectual," I wore the face of doubt earnestly, and used it as a mask for the pride that became more and more puffed up by achievement and selfishness. I had felt, for the most part, misunderstood growing up in the church, and now that I had found meaning and identity in Art, my Christian faith and my vocation as a musician were at direct odds. I remember one vivid moment attending a large Christian worship service hearing thousands praise God, and feeling entirely isolated and absolutely unable to hand over Lordship of my life to Jesus.

You will find the happy conclusion of Ying's story later in the book. For the moment notice simply this. Upon her arrival in New York, Ying did what we commonly do: she began to make self-discovery (in this case self-expression, an aspect of secondary calling) into an end in itself, abandoning the enjoyment of God (primary calling) in the process. Developing her gifts began to eclipse enjoying the One who gave them. She fell, in short, into idolatry.

We all do this—whether we are athletes or restaurateurs or teachers or parents. Consider, for example, child rearing. It is one thing to receive and raise a child in humble dependence on that child's Creator—much as a gardener will receive, nourish, and cultivate a plant. It is another thing to treat a child as a piece of marble, trying to sculpt that child into an ideal in order to reassure yourself (and others) that you are a good and successful parent. It is good and right to be a faithful parent; but it is not good to be a controlling parent whose identity and sense of value are caught up in how the kids turn out.

Bad Reasons for Being in the People Business

One of the great ironies of calling is that even "full-time" Christian workers often turn their work into a God substitute. Driven by the inordinate desire to do well with people, they can make church work a higher priority than loving God and loving people.

Pastors' families are often the hardest hit. I vividly remember my wife crying with frustration when, once again, "my ministry" had gotten in the way of a family obligation. "But, Charlie, *we* are your ministry!" Oswald Chambers rightly said somewhere: "The greatest competitor of devotion to Jesus is service for him. . . . The one aim of the call of God is the satisfaction of God, not a call to do something for him."

Why do social workers and teachers burn out? Why do pastors find themselves having to admit that they really don't like their flocks very much? Pastors, social workers, and teachers choose their lines of work because of an interest in people, and yet somehow they often end up running away from people.

Part of the reason is that we make "people fixing" into a substitute god—our reason for existence, the centerpiece of our identity. This false god disappoints us, and even beats us up. People don't change all that much, they don't appreciate our efforts, and they tend to blame us, sometimes viciously, for their own problems. They do to us, in short, what we did to God when he took on our flesh to rescue us. And their response embitters us because we have chosen to depend on their responses rather than on the Lord's company.

We have confused serving people for Christ's sake (which is right) with pleasing people for ours (which is wrong). We have replaced the simple and proper call to be faithful with the complex and elusive call to be successful.

Jesus the Faithful Failure

Think of Jesus' ministry for a moment. By the end of his life, he looked like a complete failure. His movement was in ruins; his closest associates had betrayed, deserted, and denied him; his enemies were triumphant; his body and spirit were maimed beyond imagining; his example and claims were ridiculed. There was absolutely nothing to show for all that he had done, despite all the biblical promises attached to obedience. And yet, he still loved people enough to pray for his executioners' forgiveness, to welcome the repentant thief into heaven, and to see to his mother's continuing care.[1]

Why?

---

1. Think of Jesus' words from the cross: Luke 23:34, 39–43; John 19:26–27.

Because success in this life did not control him. He had never permitted people's love for him to control his love for them. He had lived instead simply and always to please his Father, and he knew that it was his Father's pleasure that he should love them. He had said, "My food is to do the will of him who sent me,"[2] and he had lived his life that way. Primary calling had, in other words, always been primary.

This does not mean that the (apparent) failure of Jesus' mission did not break his heart. We must not think that the promise of resurrection on the far side of the cross made his human losses easy, any more than the hope of heaven makes our losses easy. To think this way is to forget that he was "tempted in every way as we are, yet without sin," and that he "learned obedience through the things that he suffered."[3] (What makes him different from you and me with respect to his humanity is not that he did not experience human disappointment as acutely as we do, but that he did not sin because of it). The loss of family, friends, followers, reputation, clothing, and respect tore into him as much as the spikes did. But Jesus was willing to lose everything as long as he had his Father's love and faithfully followed his will. And that is the test for us. We properly pursue secondary calling if we are content to fail at it. And, by contrast, we know we are slipping toward idolatry when we cannot stand to fail.

Dis-Integration and Guilt

Our idolatrous hearts adversely affect self-discovery in many ways. One is that they dis-integrate us. That is, they split us

2. John 4:34.
3. Heb. 4:15; 5:8.

up on the inside. We find ourselves not simply at odds with God. We find ourselves at odds within ourselves. We say one thing and do another. We believe one way and we feel another. Our thinking is often conflicted: one minute we are convinced of one thing, the next of its opposite. Our feelings conflict as well: we find ourselves loving and hating the same person, often during a single conversation.

Why does this happen? In large part because idolatry has many objects. When we remove God from the center, we do not replace him with *one* false god; we replace him with *many*. One minute we ignore friends because we are worshiping the god of professional success; the next we are slacking off at work because we are worshiping the god of friendship. Or, perhaps, we are caught between friends—needing so much to have both of them approve of us that we become one person when we are with one of them and another person when we are with the other.

How can God call "me" when "I" am like the Gerasene demoniac, full of many different voices all clamoring for dominance? If I am genuinely a Christian, my deepest heart wants God and God's good pleasure, but there is "another law at work in the members of my body" that defies and resists the renewed direction of my heart.[4] This conflicting "law" muddies my thinking and incites me to do things I know I should not do. It welcomes twisted ways of thinking, it resonates with the lies about God and life that fill the cultural environment in which I live, it stirs up disobedience, and it tempts me to define myself by the latest fad or by what influential people say about me.

4. Paul speaks of this tension in Rom. 7:14–24.

No sooner do we succumb to the "law at work in our bodies" than guilt sets in. We find ourselves crying out with Paul, "What a wretched man I am! Who will rescue me from this body of death?"[5] And guilt shuts down our response to calling more effectively than almost anything else does. For why should I seek to know what God wants me to do with my life when I realize that I cannot, and will not, do what he wants? Why should I try to draw near to him in a life of love and service when I know how displeasing and unpleasant my company must be? The football team that is down by fifty points at half-time does not have much reason to keep trying, especially if their coach is disgusted with them.

Samantha's Story

"Samantha," a young woman of significant musical talent, despaired of life at the end of her own undergraduate years at Juilliard. She told her story at our church one Sunday morning. Here is a portion of it. (You will find the full version in the appendix.)

> I remember, around the time of my graduation in 1999, bumping into one of my professors in the elevator. She told me how graduation from college is the beginning, a commencement for many new things to come. Though her intention was good, this idea of a new beginning bothered me greatly because I was ready to fold my life and call it quits. I was tired of fruitlessly playing the piano; I was on the verge of breaking up with my boyfriend of many years. At that moment in my life, I felt my dreams were shattered and there was nothing more to live for. . . .

5. Rom. 7:24.

During the [empty and frustrating days over the next year], I began to question my life choices. I questioned my decision to go to a conservatory. Wouldn't I have been much happier meeting normal friends and normal teachers at a normal university? What kind of job could I now get with a piano performance degree? I also looked back into my past relationships and despaired over the choices I had made. Much worse than this feeling of emptiness and meaninglessness to life, there were these memories, like stains that I could not get rid of. I kept remembering all the times I had compromised my values and beliefs, rebelled and disobeyed my parents; I remembered how I hid my faith in subtle and not so subtle ways to please my teachers, friends, and significant others; how I ruthlessly pursued my own pleasures and dreams during college. Rub as hard I tried, I could not get rid of these thoughts. In fact, these memories followed me into the subway, onto the streets, into my practice room. Like a shadow the remembrances of all my misdeeds trailed behind, next to, in front of me wherever I went. I couldn't seem to run away from it; couldn't erase it.

The source of Samantha's despair was not simply, or even most fundamentally, career angst. It was guilt. The knowledge of her double life lacerated her conscience, and it followed her everywhere, even (as she puts it) "into my practice room." Guilt, not just meaninglessness, shut her down. A life that had once been focused and musically productive dried up and became confused.

Questions
for Reflection and Discussion

1. Please read again the following sentences found near the beginning of the chapter:

   • *The heart of our problem is idolatry. We take the good things that God generously gives us and turn them into God substitutes. To put it another way, we allow secondary calling (self-discovery) to eclipse primary calling (loving God) and in the process forget the Person who issues both calls.*

   Reflect on your own experience and try to recall one or two instances when you have fallen into this pattern. Try to be specific, citing particular decisions you have made or things you have done. If you have difficulty seeing it, ask a friend to help you.

2. This chapter describes a number of symptoms of calling gone bad: dis-integration and paralyzing guilt.

   • *Try to describe these symptoms in other language.*
   • *Why does idolatry lead to these things?*

- *Where have you discovered these symptoms in your own experience or in that of those you know?*

3. Reflect on Ying's and Samantha's stories. What parallels, if any, do you find in them with your experience or the experience of someone you know?

4. Read Genesis 3:7–12.

- *What, according to these verses, does a guilty conscience do to our relationships with God and with people? Why?*
- *How do the results of a bad conscience affect a healthy response to God's calling—both primary and secondary?*

5. Remembering that Jesus was "tempted in every way as we are" (Heb. 4:15), try to imagine two disappointments in Jesus' life. How would he have felt about them? How was he able to face them, and what lessons can we learn from him about facing disappointments and even failures in our own lives?

Has a nation ever changed its gods? (Yet they are not gods at all.) But my people have exchanged their Glory for worthless idols. "Be appalled at this, O heavens, and shudder with great horror," declares the Lord. "My people have committed two sins: They have forsaken me, the spring of living water, and have dug their own cisterns, broken cisterns that cannot hold water."

Jeremiah 2:11–13

10

Delusion, Loneliness, and Envy

My nephew "Jack" would on occasion bite his younger brother. One memorable excuse: "But his arm was in my mouth when my teeth were closing." The victim's wayward arm and Jack's naughty teeth were the villains of the piece—not Jack.

Thinking Too Much, or Too Little, of Ourselves

Our twisted hearts can delude us. They draw us both to love and to hate ourselves inordinately. On the one hand we welcome delusions of grandeur, or at least of innocence. Like Adam, when confronted by our waywardness we protest that we are the victim, not the "perp"—the hero, not the villain. Adults pass the buck, just like my nephew, only with greater sophistication. Scripture says that "the heart is deceitful above all things and desperately wicked: who can know it?"[1]

We lie about our greatness as readily as we do about our crimes. The racist takes pride in his genetic inheritance, neglecting to acknowledge that his ancestors (not he) are responsible for that inheritance. Forgetting that our native intelligence, good looks, athletic ability, and life opportunities are all given to us, we count ourselves superior because of them. We take pride in the clubs we join, or the groups that accept us, assuming wrongly that greatness is simply a matter of association.

We receive an award for research and "forget" to acknowledge (even to ourselves) the parents, spouse, friends, and colleagues who made it possible. We allow fame to seduce us, confusing being well-known and admired (or envied) with knowing ourselves truly and being content with what we know.[2] We resist criticism, often preferring a rose-colored version of our achievements to the truth. Or we embrace flattery (parents who spoil us rather than risk crossing us, "friends" who puff

---

1. Jer. 17:9 KJV.
2. In *True Heroism in a World of Celebrity Counterfeits* (Colorado Springs: NavPress, 1995), Richard Keyes writes at length about the culture of celebrity—in which people are "famous for being famous," not because of who they are or what they have done.

us up in order to use us, teachers so committed to protecting our self-esteem that they never critique our work). In all of these responses, we lose track of ourselves.

Delusions of worthlessness afflict us as readily as delusions of grandeur. Defining ourselves by the gifts rather than the Giver, and discovering that we are not as capable as others (there is always someone better than you are at whatever is important to you), we fall easily into self-hatred and discouragement.

At its deepest level this response, though it makes us miserable, warrants not pity but rebuke, for it is a form of unbelieving resentment toward God. Mistrustful of the wisdom and love of the One in whose hands we are being formed, we deny him the right to order our lives as he chooses.[3]

False Modesty

Our resentment often masquerades as modesty. What appears to be humility is often actually risk-aversion rooted in shame. I won't take the risk of using my gifts because I am ashamed of the "real" me—with all of my God-given limits—and there is strong likelihood that those limits will be exposed if I go public. But to be ashamed of the real me is to be angry at God for the way he made me.

I gave my first public speech in a tenth-grade English class. It was a disaster. Required to speak for three minutes, I exhausted my note cards in 30 seconds and found myself standing before my peers for the longest 150 seconds I have

3. How radically different is the attitude we find in Ps. 139: "You knit me together in my mother's womb. I praise you because I am fearfully and wonderfully made" (vv. 13–14).

ever known. When their chuckles at my speechlessness turned to pity, I thought I would die. This trauma haunted me for many years, despite the fact that I had gifts for speaking. (It still haunts me from time to time.) When in my later teens I was asked occasionally to speak publicly, I was sleepless and sick for at least twenty-four hours beforehand. I flatly refused the urgings of my high-school headmaster to speak at Class Night my senior year. As I became more accustomed to speaking, I still chose only "safe" venues.

It has taken me a long time to understand that behind my dread-saturated "modesty" was something deeper than a tenth-grade trauma. It was a form of self-serving protectionism, which was itself an expression of an ungrateful heart. Speaking was not, for me, the occasion to love people to the best of my God-given ability; nor was it the occasion to offer up gratefully to my Creator and Redeemer the fullest expression of the talents he had given to me.

Speaking, rather, was simply (or largely) about me—about me either looking good or avoiding embarrassment. If I was reasonably sure that I could get by without looking like an idiot, then I would take the gig. Otherwise I often would not. I had to be the best, and if I could not be the best—or at least look like the best—then I would keep my gifts to myself.

Resentful Stewards

Beneath my protectionism was resentment: I was denying the Creator's right to make me the way he had made me and refusing to see the particular beauty and wisdom of his workmanship. I have since determined never to turn down a speaking invitation simply because I am afraid to do it. There may be good reasons for saying no (I may not have the gifts or training or time for it), but fear is never one of them.

In the Parable of the Talents, the first steward receives five talents and the second receives two. Without comparison or resentment they set about making the most of what they have, and when the master returns, each runs to him joyfully, crying, "See—look what I have done with what you gave me!" But the third steward, mistrustful of his master, greets his return with nothing but words: "I knew that you are a hard man, harvesting where you have not sown and gathering where you have not scattered seed. So I was afraid and went out and hid your talent in the ground. See, here is what belongs to you."[4]

We are often more like the third steward than the first two. Angry at God, doubting his wisdom and kindness in ordering and limiting our lives as he does, we "bury" our talents, or at least some of them. Tragically such hoarding turns out to be unsuccessful; for not to use a gift is to lose it.

Isolation and Toxic Envy

Lying about ourselves makes us lonely. Unclear about who we really are, we hide from each other as Adam and Eve hid from each other. We live in frightened isolation, not daring to be honest about our limits and needs because we fear that we will be taken advantage of.

Healthy competition, where *your* wholehearted and thankful use of your abilities pushes me along in the wholehearted and thankful use of *mine*, begins to change into war for ego survival. My identity, no longer resting in the God who knows

4. See Matt. 25:24–28.

and loves me, becomes increasingly tied to winning. To lose to you is to lose my self, and this I cannot stand. Love and humility give way to envy and posturing, vices that take the joy out of competing and seriously compromise my ability to relate to you in a healthy way.

Sometimes envy becomes toxic, as when, in Peter Shaffer's play *Amadeus*, court composer Salieri views some of Mozart's original manuscripts. Overwhelmed by the brilliant beauty that seems to have come fresh from Mozart's mind, the lesser artist breaks forth in bitter prayer:

> *Capisco!* I know my fate. Now for the first time I feel my emptiness as Adam felt his nakedness. . . . Tonight at an inn somewhere in this city stands a giggling child who can put on paper, without actually setting down his billiard cue, casual notes which turn my most considered ones into life-less scratches. *Grazie, Signore!* You gave me the desire to serve You—which most men do not have—then saw to it the service was shameful in the ears of the server. *Grazie!* You gave me the desire to praise You—which most men do not feel—then made me mute. *Grazie tanti!* You put into me perception of the Incomparable—which most men never know!—then ensured that I would know myself forever mediocre. *Why?* . . . *What is my fault?* . . . Until this day I have pursued virtue with rigor. I have labored long hours to relieve my fellow men. I have worked and worked the talent You allowed me. You know how hard I've worked! Solely that in the end, in the practice of the art which alone makes the world comprehensible to me, I might hear Your Voice! And now I do hear it—and it says only one name: MOZART! . . . And *my* only reward—my sublime privilege—is to be the sole man alive in this time who shall clearly recognize Your Incarnation! *Grazie e grazie ancore!* So be it! From this time

we are enemies, You and I! I'll not accept this from you—*do
You hear?* . . . They say God is not mocked. I tell You, *Man*
is not mocked! . . . *I* am not mocked! . . . They say the spirit
bloweth where it listeth: I tell You NO! It must list to virtue
or not blow at all![5]

From this time forward, Salieri determines to defy God by
silencing the voice that makes him so miserable. Consumed by
his envy, he contrives and executes a plan that sends Mozart
to an early grave.

What troubles me even more than Salieri's bitter reasoning
is the fact that his reasoning makes a lot of sense to me—I have
on occasion found myself thinking this way. This resonance
between Salieri and me means one of two things: Either God
is in fact unjust in his distribution of gifts, or I, like Salieri,
possess a terribly twisted heart. That twisted heart declares:
"If I cannot be the centerpiece in God's cosmos, or at least in
some spot in his cosmos, then that cosmos does not deserve
to stand." But to make such a demand is to insist on God's
own departure, for he is the centerpiece of his cosmos and
every part of it.

5. Quoted in Os Guinness, *The Call* (Nashville: Word Publishing, 1998),
126–27.

Questions
for Reflection and Discussion

1. This chapter describes a number of symptoms of calling gone bad: (1) delusions of grandeur or innocence, (2) delusions of worthlessness, (3) ingratitude masquerading as modesty, (4) isolation in which the competition becomes the enemy, and (5) toxic envy. Try to identify at least one decision you have recently made that gives expression to one or more of these symptoms. What happened? Why?

2. Why is it so difficult to be honest about and content with our God-given limits? See whether the following passages can help you as you face your limits: Matthew 6:25–34; Philippians 4:13; James 4:1–10.

3. Is competition always wrong? (Think of sports, or family games, or academic and artistic competition.) Is it wrong to pursue excellence? If competition and the pursuit of excellence are not always wrong, what makes them good and what makes them bad?

When a man knows how to do something, he ceases being a man when he stops doing it. . . . I have only one thought: work. I paint just as I breathe. When I work, I relax; not doing anything or entertaining visitors makes me tired.

Picasso

11

Self-Sabotage
at School and Work

arlier in the book we discussed the importance of work. We noted that God designed us to discover and enjoy him as we encounter and bring order to his world through the abilities and opportunities he has given. His aim is that in the process of this joyful engagement we will come to know not only the world and him, but ourselves as well.

We have, sadly, upset this arrangement. We tend either to devalue work or to make it too important. On the one hand we make it little more than a necessary evil, whose purpose is to enable us to do something else. Or, on the other hand, we turn it into a substitute god, in which our sense of value is too tightly bound to how well we succeed at it. We live out these tendencies in many arenas—including school, sports, and the workplace.

Getting My Ticket Punched

A popular university professor once was discussing a written assignment that was shortly due from his students. Barraged by one question after another about how long the paper needed to be and how heavily it would be weighed in the semester grading, he finally said in exasperation, "Please, just write me something that you can be proud of!"

Refreshing! But it is also increasingly strange to our way of thinking. For many of us, school is little more than the ticket we must "punch" to be ushered in to the places of power, affluence, and influence. Enjoying God in the discovery of his handiwork in and around us has little to do with the undertaking.[1] Often, discovery itself (let alone discovery of God) gets short shrift. Students are driven not so much by curiosity as by grades.

Cheating is widespread—which makes perfect sense in a setting where learning has lost its intrinsic value and is largely a means to something else. If what really matters is the result

1. Ps. 19:1 cries: "The heavens declare the glory of God." Rom. 11:36 sings, "For from him and through him and to him are all things." Such is, or should be, the driving force behind all learning.

(rather than the work), then we will do only what is necessary to get the result. If I can get an A by downloading a history paper from the net and will most likely get only a C if I try to write it myself, then it's a no-brainer: Download! (Assuming, of course, that I can avoid detection.)

Parents often add to the problem. A friend who teaches high school science is alarmed by the frequency with which she discovers parents doing projects for their children, or even lying for them. She struggles as well with the pressure coming from parents to inflate grades.

Losing the Joy of Work

Success-driven education reflects a broader problem. Why do so many athletes cave in to the pressure to use physically enhancing drugs? Why do so many star athletes seem ready to shift teams, and even nations, for a bigger income? Why do we pay superstar athletes as much as we do—and why do they demand it? I am sure that there are many reasons. But the obsession with riches and fame seems to be a dominant one. It would appear that the simple joy of playing has been infected by a toxic striving for other things.

G. K. Chesterton wrote: "A man must love a thing very much if he not only practices it without any hope of fame or money, but even practices it without any hope of doing it well. . . . If a thing is worth doing, it is worth doing badly."

We applaud such an attitude, and then sadly observe that it is hard to find—not just in "those money-grubbing athletes," but in ourselves as well. The simple joy of working hard at something eludes us. Whether we are at school, on the playing field, on stage, in the boardroom, or on the net, the desperate need to "win" in some sense—to get ahead by our efforts, to define ourselves over against the competition, or just to keep up—strangles our souls.

I speak from experience when I say that not even ministers escape this. Many of us lose the joy of our task because we are not content simply to be faithful. We must have results—people giving money, people coming to our services, people liking us, people getting "fixed."

This clamor for results—however we may measure them—is a huge problem, since we spend much more time working than we spend "enjoying" the winnings that we hope to get from work. If fame and fortune are *why* we work, and, as Andy Warhol put it, we get only our fifteen minutes of fame in our lifetime, then we are bound to be frustrated. If the work itself doesn't mean much to us—if it is only what we must do in order to enjoy a few moments doing something else—then our lives will for the most part be terribly dreary.

Fat and Happy

Clamoring for results is not the only way we diminish the intrinsic value of work. We do it as well by aiming low. I spoke in the summer of 2004 with the dean of students at a top medical school. He told me with frustration and alarm of a significant national trend: "Twenty years ago, I had to caution my students not to permit work to swallow up their lives. Now things are different. All my brightest students are going into dermatology. They all just want to be happy!"

He worried about the impact of this shift on the quality of medicine.

Growing numbers of young people are choosing personal comfort over hard work as they contemplate careers. While it is wise to lean against the workaholic's pathology (success at any cost), it is neither wise nor good simply to aim at what is easy. To shoot below our capabilities devalues work just as much as using work for success does, and it reveals a limited sense of mission in our lives.

I encourage you to read David McCullough's stirring biography of John Adams.[2] There you will find a man and wife (Abigail is as remarkable a figure as her husband), both strong Christians, who made huge sacrifices for the public good. They were not content simply to be "saved" and to have a comfortable family. They spent many months apart (particularly difficult because of the depth of their friendship), frequently endured malicious public slander, made numerous (and treacherous) trips overseas—spent their lives, in other words—all for the sake of the fragile budding nation of which they were a part. Their life was not easy, but it was good. We owe them a huge debt.

One contemporary scholar argues that whereas the "besetting sin" of an earlier time was pride, it is now sloth.[3] Few people in the rising generation, it seems, want to risk any serious efforts at change for the better, either in themselves or in the world around them. Only fools take such risks in a world where nothing is certain. It has always been easier to

2. David McCullough, *John Adams* (New York: Simon and Schuster, 2001).

3. R. R. Reno speaks of this in *The Ruins of the Church: Sustaining Faith in an Age of Diminished Christianity.* See *Mars Hill Audio Journal* (Charlottesville, VA) Vol. 67, March/April 2004.

be detached than to be committed. The sad thing is that now it has also become fashionable.

But pursuing happiness can be even more deadly for self-discovery than pursuing success. Any good parent will attest to this. Of course we want our children to grow into happy adults, but we understand that happiness can come only as a result of facing and embracing life as it actually is. This discovery involves at least two undertakings—neither of which any child wants (at first): making room for others and learning new skills. Children who are not pushed out of their comfort zones never grow up.

The hyper achiever is at least headed somewhere; she is pushing on the boundaries of her giftedness, finding out what she can and cannot do. What is more, outward movement usually requires her to deal with people. And dealing with people will draw out her gifts and her flaws—both of which she needs to discover if she is truly to know herself.

Work That Kills

We can, as we have been saying, demean work in multiple ways. But we do not all deny the value of work. Some of us make work too important.

There is, of course, nothing wrong with pouring ourselves into work. God, who himself labored over the cosmos, loves freely chosen hard work. In fact he calls us to follow his example: "Six days you shall labor and do all your work."[4] But we can, and often do, expect work to bring the sort of meaning to our lives that it is not designed to deliver. This expectation

4. Ex. 20:9.

over time strips the joy from work and leaves us exhausted, anxious, and driven.

If, for example, we are serious musicians (or athletes, or parents), we may find ourselves treating music (or sport, or home-making) as if it had the power to integrate our lives or give them ultimate meaning. And this is very foolish—like a tick trying to suck blood out of a carpet, or a scuba diver trying to draw air from an empty tank. When we give our lives away to any created thing—however good that thing is—we begin to die on the inside. We become frustrated when the thing we depend on stops "delivering" the charge, or sense of meaning, it once delivered. We scramble desperately to recapture that "great family vacation" or "that moment" when music, performer, and audience came together as one, or that "sweet victory" when the team was in sync down to the final whistle.

So obsessed can we become with our futile quest that we lose touch with people, or perhaps even drive them away. So obsessed can we become trying to find life in this one thing that we lose the ability to find life in the richness that God has poured into the world. Our creative works cease to be expansive expressions of love, efforts to share something beautiful with others. Instead they become sterile and self-serving—*my* performance, *my* technique, *my* success, *my* parenting, *my* identity. We lose the ability genuinely to enjoy and celebrate other people's gifts, joys, and successes. Our lives, rather than expanding in the enjoyment of life and work, actually shrink down.

Two Very Different Artists

Pablo Picasso said: "When a man knows how to do something, he ceases being a man when he stops doing it. . . . I have only one thought: work. I paint just as I breathe. When I work, I relax; not doing anything or entertaining visitors makes me tired." He also said: "When I die, it will be a shipwreck, and as when a huge ship sinks, many people all around will be sucked down with it."

His single-mindedness, at first glance so appealing, fed a life that, according to mistress Dora Maar, controlled people but could not love them. Three people committed suicide when he died in 1973.[5] Picasso was a creative genius who worshipped his work. And that worship made him both obsessive and cruel.

J. S. Bach was also a creative genius—but of a very different sort. One of the most brilliant and prolific composers of all time, he seems to have seen himself not as some kind of a god, but as a workman in the craft that God had given him, often writing "SDG" (Latin initials for the phrase *Soli Deo Gloria*—"To God alone be glory") at the end of his compositions. His life was very real—full of children, of discouragements, of deadlines (a cantata a week!), and nothing like the recognition he is accorded today. (Mendelssohn brought him to the world's attention many years after his death.) Because his view of himself was not overblown, he was able just to carry on, day by day, in the work before him.

People who understand that their creativity is a gift of God, rather than putting it in the place of God himself, discover

5. The quotes and analysis are found in Os Guinness, *The Call* (Nashville: Word Publishing, 1998), 88–89, 242.

a paradoxical freedom. They are both free *to* work and free *from* work. Motivated by love and gratitude (powerful motivators) they are free to work very hard, giving their best back to God. At the same time, because they know that neither they nor their work is God, they are free from the burden of taking themselves or their work too seriously—as if their giftedness mandated perfection.

Questions
for Reflection and Discussion

1. Bosses and circumstances can make work miserable for us. But we can make ourselves miserable at work as well. How do your attitudes toward school or work adversely affect your joy at school or work?

2. Do you tend more toward "clamoring for results" or toward laziness? In what specific ways does your tendency assert itself? How does it reflect a diminished view of God's ideal for work? How does it inhibit self-discovery? What makes it idolatrous?

3. Have you "shot low" in your career aspirations? If so, why? Do you think there are good, God-honoring reasons for aiming low? If so, what are they?

4. Compare Bach's and Picasso's approaches to their work. How are they different? In what ways are you more like Bach? In what ways are you more like Picasso?

5. Jesus said, "I came that they may have life and have it abundantly" (John 10:10). David wrote, "In your presence there is fullness of joy" (Ps. 16:11). What do you do for the simple joy of doing it? What is it, and why do you enjoy it?

4

Redemption
Help along the Way

"It means," said Aslan, "that though the Witch knew the Deep Magic, there is a magic deeper still which she did not know. Her knowledge goes back only to the dawn of time. But if she could have looked a little further back, into the stillness and the darkness before Time dawned, she would have read there a different incantation. She would have known that when a willing victim who had committed no treachery was killed in a traitor's stead, the Table would crack and Death itself would start working backward."

C. S. Lewis, *The Lion, the Witch and the Wardrobe*

12

A Safe Identity

was speaking recently with a young friend struggling to make it in the world of theater and film. He was depressed—not just because he was finding it hard to get work, but because of the selfishness he was beginning to discover in himself. "I'm so arrogant when I get work and so mean to those I love when I don't. Why can't I just do my best and not be so controlled by how successful I am?"

The reality of the Fall can (and does) make the pursuit of calling very discouraging. Thankfully, the Fall is not the only reality at work, for we live in the day of the King. At the outset of his public ministry Jesus proclaimed, "Repent, for the kingdom of God is at hand." To paraphrase: "Change your thinking! Change your lives! The King has landed in enemy territory and is retaking the land. He has come to roll back all that is wrong in and around us—and nothing can stop him!"

In other words, Redemption is afoot—death is starting to work backward. Redemption is the third Big Idea we discuss in this book. What follows is a summary of the meaning of this idea as it relates to the pursuit of calling.

Christ, the Second Adam, is presently at work fixing everything that the Fall has marred—everything that is wrong in me, in society, in the natural order, and in my relationship with God. By his holy life and sacrificial death he has fully and eternally reconciled me to God. Completely safe with God, I can look without fear at who I really am—at my limits and my twistedness. Safe with God, I do not have to justify my existence by performance or by lying about myself. Safe with God, I no longer need to be defined or controlled by people or circumstances. Indwelt by the resurrected Christ, I have power to change dramatically: to re-integrate myself, to love people without fear, to express my giftedness with simple joy rather than isolating arrogance, and to admit my limits with contentment. Safe in God and indwelt by his Spirit, I can work hard, courageously, and hopefully to help others hear and respond to God's call.

A New Way of Thinking about Myself

How do we permit the reality of King Jesus' present reign to work its way practically into our quest to know and be ourselves? By daily repentance. This may sound rather dreary, like the monks in the Monte Python film who chant, "Pie, Jesu, Domine" as they systematically beat each other with whips. But it is not.

To repent does not mean to beat myself up or to try to make myself feel bad. It means to change my mind. It means to stop seeing things one way and to start seeing them another way, regardless of how I may feel or how things may look, and then to order my life around this new way of seeing. Repentance is crucial for transformation—which is why Jesus begins his preaching with that word and why the apostle Paul wrote, "Do not be conformed to this world, but be transformed by the renewal of your mind."[1]

We will devote the next three chapters to four new ways of thinking and the mission that flows from that new vision. We must, and can, change our thinking: (1) about what makes us safe, (2) about what defines us, (3) about change in ourselves, and (4) about change in our world.

Who or What Makes Me Safe?

Consider the first of these. The finished work of my Redeemer means that I am both fully known and completely safe with God. Joyfully embracing this, not just once but habitually, opens the way to renewed self-discovery.

Let me explain. With people I am usually either safe or known—but rarely both at the same time. I am safe, in other words, because they don't know the real truth about me. If I were to let people in on everything that there is to know about me, I would become their hostage—both because I have some very ugly stuff inside and because people are cruel.

1. Rom. 12:2 ESV.

This is why Adam and Eve tried to cover themselves with fig leaves. Prior to the Fall they were naked and unashamed; but after the Fall, vulnerability became too risky. And things were even worse with God—not because God is cruel, but because he is honest (he will never lie about us) and good (he cannot tolerate evil) and he sees absolutely everything. We can cover up with one another, but we cannot cover up with God. "The heart is deceitful above all things and beyond cure. Who can understand it? I the LORD search the heart."[2]

Fully Known and Completely Safe with Jesus

Jesus changes all this. Because of him my relationship with God is very different from my relationship with other people. With, and because of, Jesus the Redeemer I am both fully known and completely safe. At the cross, Jesus met me at my very worst. For at that mysterious moment all my toxic envy, all my deceit, all my secret sins, all my ingratitude, all my self-centered neglect and cruelty—everything that is corrupt and twisted about my attitudes and my behavior—was exposed to the full heat of God's justice, attached to Jesus, and punished: "We all, like sheep, have gone astray, each of us has turned to his own way; and the LORD has laid on him the iniquity of us all."[3]

By fully identifying with our sin and then being punished for it, Jesus satisfied God's justice. Precisely how this identification works is a mystery. But the Bible guarantees that it happened; and its meaning is liberating. Not only *will* God

2. Jer. 17:9.
3. Isa. 53:6.

no longer condemn us; but he *cannot* do so—not without committing a great injustice. The God of all justice would never punish a person twice for the same crime, and he has already punished me in Christ. This is why Paul writes, "Therefore, there is now no condemnation for those who are in Christ Jesus."[4]

Let me drive this home with the words of theologian John Murray:

> There was only one, and there will not need to be another, who bore the full weight of the divine judgment upon sin and bore it so as to end it. The lost will eternally suffer in the satisfaction of justice. But they will never satisfy it. Christ *satisfied* justice. . . . He bore the unrelieved and unmitigated damnation of sin, and he *finished* it. . . . This is the explanation of Gethsemane with its bloody sweat and agonizing cry, "O, my Father, if it be possible let this cup pass from me" (Matthew 26:39). And this is the explanation of the most mysterious utterance that ever ascended from earth to heaven, "My God, my God, why have you forsaken me?" . . . Perish the presumption that dares to speak of *our* Gethsemanies and *our* Calvaries! It is trifling with the most solemn spectacle in all history, a spectacle unparalleled, unique, unrepeated and unrepeatable. . . . Here we are spectators of a wonder the praise and glory of which eternity will not exhaust. It is the Lord of glory, the Son of God incarnate, the God-man, drinking the cup given him by the eternal Father, the cup of woe and indescribable agony. . . . It is God in our nature forsaken by God.[5]

4. Rom. 8:1.
5. John Murray, *Redemption: Accomplished and Applied* (Grand Rapids: Eerdmans, 1970), 77 (italics mine).

Jesus satisfied justice. There cannot, therefore, be an ounce of condemnation left in the heart of God toward you if you belong to Jesus by faith.

A New Foundation for Self-Discovery

What does all this have to do with calling? It provides us with the indispensable foundation for renewed self-discovery and self-expression. For it makes me comprehensively and eternally safe. No person and no circumstance can, in the final analysis, hurt me.

Dietrich Bonhoeffer was a German pastor whom the Nazis imprisoned for his involvement in a plot to assassinate Adolf Hitler. The following poem, which he wrote in prison, describes the life-changing hope that the gospel gave him.[6]

Who Am I?
Who am I? They often tell me
I would step from my cell's confinement
Calmly, cheerfully, firmly,
Like a squire from his country house.
Who am I? They often tell me
I used to speak to my warders
Freely, friendly, clearly,
As though it were mine to command.
Who am I? They also tell me
I bore the day's misfortune
Equably, smilingly, proudly,
Like one accustomed to win.

6. Reprinted with the permission of Scribner, an imprint of Simon and Schuster Adult Publishing Group, from *Letters and Papers from Prison, Revised, Enlarged Edition* by Dietrich Bonhoeffer. Copyright 1953, 1967, 1971 by SCM Press Ltd. All rights reserved.

Am I then really all that which men tell of?
Or am I only what I myself know of myself,
Restless and longing and sick, like a bird in a cage,
Struggling for breath, as though hands were compressing
    my throat,
Yearning for colors, for flowers, for the voices of birds,
Thirsting for words of kindness, for neighborliness,
Trembling with anger at despotisms and petty humiliation,
Tossing in expectation of great events,
Powerlessly trembling for friends at an infinite distance,
Weary and empty at praying, at thinking, at making,
Faint, and ready to say farewell to it all?
Who am I? This or the other?
Am I one person today, and tomorrow another?
Am I both at once? A hypocrite before others,
And before myself a contemptibly woebegone weakling?
Or is something within me still like a beaten army,
Fleeing in disorder from victory already achieved?
Who am I? They mock me, these lonely questions of mine.
Whoever I am, thou knowest, O God, I am thine!

Bonhoeffer's world was still fallen. The poem makes clear that his faith did not magically erase his internal struggles. Nor did his faith deliver him from the Nazis: he was executed shortly before the Allies liberated his prison. Nevertheless, Bonhoeffer was profoundly free. He knew that God knew everything about him—his doubts, his hypocrisy, his sins—and still loved him. He was safe in God's arms. No troubled thought or difficult circumstance (not even death) could alter the truth of his final ringing affirmation: "Whoever I am, thou knowest, O God, I am thine!" It is difficult to imagine Bonhoeffer writing the poem at all, or writing with such honesty, or exercising such graciousness toward his captors, were that affirmation not rooted in his heart.

I will never begin to know myself until I can face myself. I will never be able to begin to unscramble the web of interior contradiction unless I am confident that, no matter how scrambled and ugly things are inside, I am safe, loved, and on the road to full recovery. I will never be able to open myself to people, and I will never be able to take the risks of love (risks without which I will never discover who I am), until I no longer need people for my deepest validation. The gospel frees me from that need. Plenty about me may shock people, but nothing can shock God, and all of it has been covered by the cross.

Who or What Defines Me?

When left to our own devices we will tend to define ourselves and each other much too narrowly. We sometimes say, "She is Asian-American," or "He is African-American," as if such terms give us the key that unlocks that person's deepest secrets. And we do this, not only with unchangeable endowments (such as race), but also with characteristics that arise, at least in part, from choices people make: we say so-and-so is "gay," or "Republican," or "rich," assuming that by such terms we have gotten to their essence somehow. People who wrestle with eating disorders find their sense of self is clarifying or disintegrating depending on their weight.

Part of what drives us to shrink people (including ourselves) in these ways is fear that our lives will have no meaning if we don't define them ourselves. We know that we cannot take in the whole of our identity, and we are afraid that whatever we are now may change dramatically in five years. And so, we try desperately to find something specific or measurable that will identify us. It may be something that we latch on to because, in the face of so many uncontrollable things, we can at least control this. Or it may be something we can do that sets us apart. Or it may be something we have inherited (our race, our skills, our looks) that distances us from certain groups while identifying ourselves with others.

We are, in other words, in charge of our identity. Or so we think. The sad fact is that we are not. If we try to define ourselves by something we think we can control (our weight, our children's development, our creative output), or by some special talent or genetic endowment we happen to possess, that thing will inevitably begin to control us.

Roberta's Story

What follows is a part of the story that "Roberta" told at our church.

> I am thankful that I am blessed with Christian parents and a family with solid roots. I have believed in Jesus for as long as I can remember. In fact, growing up, I asked Jesus into my heart several times, wanting to make sure God knew I was serious. Even still, when it came time silently to confess our sins in the congregational prayer, I couldn't think of much to say. After all, I knew I was a good kid, and I seemed to get along with most people pretty well. This is a pretty accurate picture of how I stayed until I graduated from high school: a happy, healthy person thinking I was doing pretty well at measuring up to God's standard for me.

When I came to New York four years ago for college, one of the first things that struck me about the city was how many beautiful people there were everywhere. I began to compare my physical appearance to every woman I passed on the street, feeling either good or depressed by how I physically measured up to others. I wanted to be a picture of perfection, and I thought that as long as I maintained a good image, I could achieve that.

This desire consumed me, and I held myself rigidly to not overeating. As long as I wasn't eating a bite past full, I thought God was pleased with me and I actually believed I was without sin. In my mind, my salvation dangled over how I ate. I feared that overeating would cause me to lose my apparent good favor with God and cause me to lose my salvation. For a few months, I thought I had achieved my goals for perfection. I felt good about how I looked, I was a leader for the Juilliard Christian Fellowship, and I had started dating the man I am soon to marry. I prided myself in being able to not overeat, and my mind was a judgmental commentary about how others were sinning all around me. I am amazed that I still thought I was without sin even while entertaining these thoughts.

When I went home for break after my sophomore year, my family noticed that I was not eating as I normally did. My sister caught me throwing up my dinner when I thought no one was watching. What followed was a hard time of admitting to myself and my family that I was not healthy. I was struggling with anorexia and bulimia, behaviors that were consumed by my desire to be thin, pretty, and perfect.

With the help of my family and fiancé, God did bring me through that period of my life, and last year I started eating regularly again. I returned to my normal weight, and what followed was an overwhelming depression. You see, I had not replaced my *image* of God with the *real* God, and I felt empty and without purpose. I knew God was there loving me, and I wanted to submit my life to him, but I could not let go of my own desire for perfection. I started taking anti-depressants, which failed to help. I remember wanting to die, feeling like I had no reason for staying on earth, that nobody would care if I just vanished.

I couldn't have been more wrong! Psalm 18 says:

The ropes of death surrounded me; the floods of destruction swept over me. The grave wrapped its ropes around me; death itself stared me in the face. But in my distress I cried out to the LORD; yes, I prayed to my God for help. He heard me from his sanctuary; my cry reached his ears. He reached down from heaven and rescued me; he drew me out of deep waters. He delivered me from my powerful enemies, from those who hated me and were too strong for me. They attacked me at a moment when I was weakest, but the LORD upheld me. He led me to a place of safety; he rescued me because he delights in me.[7]

This last year God has slowly showed me how wrong I was in my view of salvation—that in fact, as his child, I cannot lose my salvation. I thought that by achieving the perfect image, I could accomplish what only one man, Jesus Christ, could ever accomplish. When I realize that even my best efforts fall so short of God's standard for me, what a relief to know that my sins are already covered; that God's wrath that

7. New Living Translation, 2nd ed., Ps. 18:4–6, 16–19 (Carol Stream, IL: Tyndale, 2005).

should have been poured out on *me* in my pride, selfishness, and arrogance has already been poured out on *Christ* for my sake. Instead of living with the pressure of trying to earn my way to heaven and the fear of losing my salvation in the process, I can rest in God's hands. My salvation has already been earned and paid for, and there is nothing I can do to add to that.

Healing and Proper Identity

"Roberta" discovered that defining herself, in her case by how much she weighed and how pretty she looked, made her miserable (a problem exacerbated by living in New York, where there is always someone who is prettier and slimmer than you are). She became a slave to the image she had created for herself—an image that drove her to deceive her family and harm her body. Worse, ugly and isolating attitudes began to surface. Blind to her own flaws, she became hypercritical of others, judging them relentlessly. Not even coming clean about her eating disorder helped. In fact honesty only made things worse, because it stripped from her the pattern of behavior that had given her life its meaning. Suicide became a real option.

Healing began for Roberta when she started to see that living up to an image she had created for herself could never "save" her. She simply could not keep up with the image. She began to discover that God was not a taskmaster, but a Savior who had already addressed her real issues (her pride, selfishness, and arrogance) at immense cost to himself. She began to discover that Jesus had fulfilled on her behalf everything necessary for her to find her true self in the arms of God.

Though Roberta does not make this explicit, she began to discover something else. She began to discover that creating her own persona has nothing to do with salvation: it is like running a race on the wrong course—a grueling trek with no possibility of reward. What she really wanted, and what she really needed, was to find the real God and to discover that, whoever she is, her identity is safe with him. And this has begun. She will continue to struggle, as we all do, with identity issues, but death has really begun to "work backward" in her thanks to Christ, the Second Adam.

Questions
for Reflection and Discussion

1. Read over the summary of the Big Idea of Redemption in the box near the beginning of the chapter.

   - *What aspects of the summary are new to you?*
   - *Which are confusing or difficult to believe? Why?*
   - *Which are comforting? Why?*
   - *Which are challenging? Why?*

2. Read over the statement by John Murray near the beginning of the chapter. What does he mean when he says that Jesus *satisfied* justice? How does this satisfaction of justice provide us with the "indispensable foundation for renewed self-discovery and self-expression"?

3. Do you feel completely safe with God? Why or why not?

4. Discuss or reflect on this statement: "Jesus may make me safe with God 'eternally.' But that safety is no guarantee

that people and circumstances this side of death won't hurt me. So what good is it?"

5. List one or two ways in which you have tried to define yourself. In what ways have you found trying to define yourself to be the cause of pain (to yourself or to other people), or at least frustrating?

Therefore, if anyone is in Christ, he is a new creation; the old has gone, the new has come!

2 Corinthians 5:17

13

A New Trajectory

Roberta's story in the previous chapter encourages us. And it does so not simply because it tells of the comprehensive forgiveness that the Second Adam brings. It encourages us because it shows Roberta actually changing—overcoming her eating disorder and working her way through deep depression.

To be forgiven and safe with God is necessary, but it does not fully satisfy us. We want to change. We need to be better people—truly admirable people. We want in some ways to be like Sydney Carton, the character who changes dramatically over the course of Charles Dickens' *A Tale of Two Cities*. Weary of a wasteful, selfish life, he rescues a rival from prison on the eve of his execution, drugging and then trading places with him. (The two men look alike.) As he approaches the guillotine the next morning, he utters with deep satisfaction, "It is a far, far better thing that I do than I have ever done."

We may wonder whether we would have Sydney Carton's courage in similar circumstances. But we long to share his satisfaction. We want to be able to look back on our lives, content that we have learned to love well, that we have learned to be wise and noble people.

The comforting thing is that our Redeemer also desires this for us. It is not enough, even for him, that we should simply be forgiven and safe. He wants to be able to say to us at the end of our days, "Well done, good and faithful servant. You have been faithful over a little. I will put you over much. Enter now the joy of your master."

He wants to call us "good." He wants to call us "faithful." He wants us to be his colleagues, and therefore to share his joy, in having advanced the things that matter to him.

Arranging Our Circumstances

So deeply committed is our Redeemer to this goal that he bends his all-controlling and mysterious power to it, working all things "together for good to them that love God, to them who are the called according to his purpose."[1] "John," a law student in our congregation who at one point thought he had lost a semester of work when his computer crashed, told

---

1. Rom. 8:28 KJV.

us one Sunday morning about what he had begun to learn through the experience:

> God managed to show his love for me in a very funny way. When I wondered why God had placed me through this ordeal, I think he answered me quite clearly after the wreckage was cleared away. God seemed to say, "I knew all along just how weak your faith was. But *you* had no idea. You knew abstractly that my love for you doesn't at all depend on what you're capable of. This trial let you see more concretely that I love you despite your weaknesses, that I love you as if you have no flaws. My Son Jesus has made you perfect in my eyes. Your computer crashed so that you could see these things. And aren't you glad it happened?"

> No way! But I couldn't imagine a better way of having learned these things.

> Obviously, there is nothing at all that feels very tender or nurturing about experiencing difficulties. No, what God uses to show his love for us sometimes causes many tears, much fright, and much hurt. Growing closer to God, the thing a Christian wants most, is wrought with something people want least: pain. . . .

> To be honest, part of me is still afraid of how God will answer my prayers for him to strengthen my faith. But now I have a better idea of who God is. And I trust him more. I trust his purposes more. I realize that I've got too many broken things within me, like doubts, insecurities, and selfish tendencies, that he still needs to fix. You've probably heard the verse "God disciplines those he loves." And I know he loves me far too much to let me go on as I am now.

John has been discovering that the Redeemer who died for his forgiveness also lives for his transformation. He has been discovering that his Redeemer uses everything, including (and even especially) hardship, for his good. He is learning, in other words, that the God who loves him may not always be gentle with him, but that the shake-ups in his life, just as much as the moments of serenity, are all part of a beautiful tapestry that God is weaving in John's life. The Second Adam is our powerful Friend, into whose wise hands God has placed all things, for our good.

Inside Help

All this is plenty comforting. But there is even more—and we need more. It is not enough to have a friend ordering our circumstances. We need this friend walking alongside us as we make our way. More than that, we need this friend inside us, changing our motives and removing our fears, so that we learn to grow through the sometimes traumatic circumstances he orders up. Without insider help we are simply too weak—like mountaineers without food. We may have the best guide in the world, and a clearly marked trail, but we lack the nourishment to climb.

To use the language of the Bible, we need "living hope"[2]—a hope that is alive and powerful—powerful enough to keep us pressing on against all the forces of self-sabotage we have been discussing. The Second Adam gives us this hope because he lives in us. He is "Christ in us, the hope of glory." He is the "new creation" who has replaced the old me with a new me.

2. See 1 Peter 1:3.

He is the faithful One who will not fail to complete on the last day the "good work" that he began in us.[3]

Here is what I am saying. The crucifixion was the heart of Christ's work, but it was not the end of it. He rose from the dead and on Pentecost poured out his Spirit forever upon his church. And his Holy Spirit makes everything different in our experience. He brings the goodness of Jesus into us. He changes our inner appetites so that we begin genuinely to love the things that God loves and to hate the things that God hates. He brings the future glories of heaven into our present life, not in their fullness, but truly.

If you are a Christian this means that at that secret place deep at your center, you are profoundly and everlastingly different. The "old you" is still there, but there is a new you—someone who loves to love God—and that new you, though often hidden like a spring shoot under piles of dead leaves, is the real you. And that real you is going to survive and eventually make its way to the light of day.

Clinging to Reality

In our corporate worship, we sometimes sing this song:

> I will give you all my worship,
> I will give you all my praise,
> You alone I long to worship,
> You alone are worthy of my praise![4]

3. See Col. 1:27; 2 Cor. 5:17; Phil. 1:6.
4. From "You're Worthy of My Praise" by David Ruis. Copyright 1991, Shade Tree Music (Administered by Music Services on behalf of Maranatha Praise, Inc.) and Maranatha Praise, Inc./ASCAP (Administered by Music Services). All rights reserved. Used by permission.

These words have at times bothered me: no one gives God *all* his worship and *all* his praise. But as I have sung them in the light of what we have been saying about newness, I have seen something else. And that vision has led me more than once to pray aloud before the congregation something like this at the conclusion of the song:

> Dear Lord, you know better than we do that, in one sense, these words are not true. We sing them with great religious feeling perhaps, but we don't live them. There are all sorts of things that we love more than we love you. This song condemns us. But there is another sense, gracious Redeemer, in which these words are in fact profoundly true of us. They are true because you have sent your Spirit to live in us—and there is no question but that *he* loves you this way. We praise you, dear Lord, that you are at work in us and that it is only a matter of time before you finish what you have begun.

We looked in chapter 12 at the importance of repenting—of changing our thinking now that Jesus the King has come into our world. Here is one of the ways we need to repent: we need to repent of expecting so little of ourselves.

In our own day it has become fashionable to be cynical—to withdraw into self-protective irony. We need to preach daily to ourselves, "You do not *have* to envy or be afraid of the competition, you don't *have* to be obsessed by grades or promotions or weight, you don't *have* to be bitter because you are not as smart or as good looking as so-and-so, you do not *have* to be in control, you don't *have* to be joyless before God. You can change—and you will—for Jesus is alive and with you!"

A Story

I have a friend who has had a very difficult life. She is lonely, in chronic pain, and at times so afraid that she has difficulty breathing. Life often seems so pointless and unfair that she slides into bitterness and despair, comparing her lot with that of others and wondering why she should continue to live. But she also prays for me and for others, including those whom she feels have offended her. She routinely asks how I am doing, she diligently takes notes whenever we talk, and she listens to sermon tapes and goes back to the Bible again and again.

Once when her fears were making it difficult for her to breathe, I asked her, "What do you know is true about you?" She gasped out, staccato fashion, in response: "Jesus loves me. . . . Jesus died for me. . . . I am forgiven. . . . Jesus rose from the dead for me. . . . Jesus prays for me. . . . He is with me. . . . My body belongs to him. . . . He will give me a new body one day. . . ."

Her answer stunned me. It did so in the first place because I knew that she could never have made those affirmations so clearly a year or two earlier. She had really changed, even if she was too close to herself to see the change. Her answer also stunned me because I knew that none of these assertions was a platitude for her. Each was (and is) a hard-won conviction that is tested every day of her life. She forgets them at times in the midst of her pain and frustration, but she keeps coming back to them.

Why? Because she is not alone in her battle, even if she thinks she is. She is a new creature, made alive by the Redeemer who lives in and with her. Christ is in her, the hope of glory.

Questions
for Reflection and Discussion

1. What is the difference between envy and admiration? Think of someone whom you admire. What is it about that person that you admire, and how do you try to emulate it? If you do not try to be like that person, why don't you?

2. We read in this chapter that Jesus our redeemer desires to be able to praise us for being good and faithful, that he wants us to share in his joy over a life well lived. Do you have difficulty believing this? If so, why?

3. In his story "John" says: "Growing closer to God, the thing a Christian wants most, is wrought with something people want least: pain." How has your Redeemer used pain to change you?

4. What is meant in this chapter by the statement, "We need to repent of expecting so little of ourselves"?

   • *Do you tend to expect too little of yourself? If so, why?*

- *Read Ezekiel 36:26–28 and 2 Corinthians 5:17. How do they help you improve your expectations?*
- *Where do you see evidence of the truth of these passages in your experience?*

5. Spend some time in prayer, using Philippians 1:6 and 2 Corinthians 5:17 as the basis for both petition and praise in the light of one or two recurring problems with which you struggle.

This, then, is how you should pray: "Our Father in heaven, hallowed be your name, your kingdom come, your will be done on earth as it is in heaven."

Jesus, Matthew 6:9–10

14

It's Not Just about Me

spoke once at a large campus fellowship meeting at a university in New York. My topic was "shalom"—the holistic "peace" that Jesus came to bring. I was struck as I joined in the extended time of singing before I spoke by how much at odds the texts we were singing were with the talk I was about to give. Every song was about private piety—about *my* worship, *my* trials, *my* surrender, *my* joy and dedication. One song was particularly striking. Its principal text was Isaiah 9:6: "For to us a child is born, to us a son is given, and the government will be on his shoulders. And he will be called Wonderful Counselor, Mighty God, Everlasting Father, Prince of Peace."

But the text of Isaiah 9:6 had been curiously modified, so that what we kept singing was "You are *my* counselor, you are *my* prince of peace." By the insertion of "my" into "Prince of Peace," the essential and profound meaning of the text was all but removed. We were singing, "Jesus, you have come to give me a personal experience of peace in the midst of my trials and my struggles with guilt." This reality may be true (it is), but it is not the reality about which the passage is concerned. The picture we have there is that God will send his Son into the world to bring *shalom*.

The Vision of Shalom

Consider the rich meaning of *shalom*. The term covers much more ground than our word *peace*. To look for shalom is to look for harmony everywhere—between people and nations, between people and nature, in the natural order, between creatures and their Creator. We catch glimpses of it when a friend who has been at death's door is restored to us, when a war ends, when we apologize to someone and the relationship is restored, when a pair of figure skaters dance a perfect routine, or when a number of companies band together to make a burnt-out section of their city lovely and affordable.

We felt the power of shalom as German citizens danced for joy on the crumbling remains of the Berlin Wall. We saw it on the screen when Oskar Schindler sacrificed his fortune to rescue his Jewish workers from Auschwitz. We felt it when apartheid ended bloodlessly in South Africa and when the Reconciliation

Commission was erected to address the injustice that had been committed under the old regime. We long for shalom when we see landscapes destroyed by strip mining and lifeless creatures at the seashore caked in the debris of an oil spill.

Cornelius Plantinga imagines, in contemporary terms, what it would be like if shalom were to fill our world:

> Nations and races . . . would treasure differences in other nations and races as attractive, important, complementary. . . .
>
> Business associates would rejoice in one another's promotions. . . . All around the world, people would stimulate and encourage one another's virtues. Newspapers would be filled with well-written accounts of acts of great moral beauty, and, at the end of the day, people on their porches would read these and savor them and call to each other about them.
>
> Above all . . . God would preside in the unspeakable beauty for which human beings long and in the mystery of holiness that draws human worship like a magnet. In turn, each human being would reflect and color the light of God's presence out of the inimitable resources of his or her own character and essence. Human communities would present their ethnic and regional specialties to other communities in the name of God, in glad recognition that God, too, is a radiant and hospitable community, of three persons. In their own accents, communities would express praise, courtesies, and deferences that, when massed together, would keep building like waves of a passion that is never spent.[1]

1. Cornelius Plantinga, *Not the Way It's Supposed to Be* (Grand Rapids: Eerdmans, 1995), 11–12.

This, or some even more splendidly satisfying version of it, is what the Second Adam lived, died, and rose again to accomplish. And it is what he is presently at work creating.

Shalom and Calling

What does all this have to do with calling? A great deal. We might put it this way: if the Caller is busily at work restoring harmony everywhere, then I must be involved in that task wherever he has placed me. For I will know myself only as I labor alongside my Maker. In other words, our pursuit of calling needs to fit into the Caller's larger plan. And that plan is not simply about *my* renewal. It is about the renewal of *everything*.

To put it yet another way, we need to repent of our despair about the world. We need to change our thinking in the light of Jesus' work. Things may be changing slowly, but they are changing. We will have to wait until Christ returns before shalom comes in fullness, but shalom has begun. This is why Paul writes, "For we know that the whole creation has been groaning together in the pains of childbirth *until now*." It is why he also writes, "If anyone is in Christ, [there is] *a new creation*."[2] Notice Paul's choice of words—"new creation," not simply "new creature." It is not simply that I have a new heart if I am in Christ; it is that I have been brought by Christ into a new order of things.

While we must patiently await shalom's full expression (as we'll see in the chapters on consummation), we can expect and should work for glimpses of it now. We believe this because Jesus has been raised from the dead and is now ruling at

2. Rom. 8:22; 2 Cor. 5:17.

God's right hand. He has already begun to push his "shalom" agenda.

Renewing Our Vision

Practically speaking, this means at least two things. First, we need to train our eyes to see his renewing handiwork. It is everywhere. Think about it. Did you have to forego your desire to play football or to pursue the violin during your high school years because you needed to work to keep food on the table? Chances are you did not. Do you have a job that you actually enjoy most of the time? More and more people do, at least in western culture. Are you contemplating a number of good and interesting job possibilities, rather than scrounging to get anything at all so that you can pay the heating bill this winter? Have you ever experienced successful surgery or had a strep infection killed off by antibiotics? Are you being paid a livable wage? If your answer is yes to any of these questions, then you are benefiting from the work of the Redeemer.

Think more broadly. Do you live in a society in which those who are stronger than you are not free to do whatever they want to you—where you can contest an injustice and not be killed (and perhaps can even win the contest)? Do you study in an environment where you are free to speak your mind without censure, even if you hold a point of view that is new or out of fashion? Do you live in a country where you are free to worship as your conscience dictates? Do you enjoy music, literature, and art whose creators would never have been able to produce those works but for a high level of social and economic stability?

Have you ever had the satisfaction of seeing genocidal war criminals brought to justice? Have you ever seen research and public policy combine to improve public health? Have you ever rejoiced at the overthrow of unjust labor practices or at the decrease in homelessness and joblessness in your town? Are there tracts of land in your state or country that are legally protected from development? Has your state or country grappled over how much greenhouse gas may be discharged into the atmosphere?

What we need to see is that all these sorts of things—improved healthcare and quality of life, the rule of law, economic prosperity, care for the environment, the patronage of the arts—do not happen just by chance. They are fruits of Jesus' reign. We see them this way, not because we can always see the historical connection between the rise of Christianity and these benefits (though the connection is often very strong[3]), nor because the church has always championed them (there have been some dark moments), nor because those who promote them consciously honor Jesus (environmental advocates are as likely to be atheists as they are to be theists). We see these benefits as the fruits of Jesus' reign, rather, because we have been let in on a cosmic secret: "For God was pleased . . . through [Christ] to reconcile to himself all things, whether things on earth or things in heaven, by making peace through his blood, shed on the cross."[4]

Jesus Christ is God's appointed reconciler. His healing hand has begun to stretch everywhere. His healing presence

3. See Vincent Carroll and David Shiflett, *Christianity on Trial: Arguments Against Anti-Religious Bigotry* (San Francisco: Encounter Books, 2002). The authors document the astonishing degree to which so many good things that we enjoy have arisen from the impact of the gospel on our world.
4. Col. 1:19–20.

shines on in our still-broken world like an unquenchable candle in a dark and drafty room. He is always giving us glimpses of what is to come—if only we have the eyes to see them.

On Mission

Armed with our insight into what the King is doing in our world, we will undertake a second task. We will embark on a mission. That mission will *not* primarily be to figure ourselves out (God promises to take care of that); it will be rather to help our neighbors figure themselves out. In other words, we who are disciples of the Second Adam have a special task, a special calling, in the present age—and that calling is to help our neighbors hear the voice, and see the hand, of God.

This mission involves two parts. One part is evangelism, in which we tell our friends how they can safely hear and obey the voice of their Maker. We say that we believe in a God who calls. But to say that without ever articulating our God's words of welcome to our friends is not to practice what we preach. We are not all, like Billy Graham, called to be full-time evangelists. But we are all called to love our friends, and if we really love them we will want them truly to find themselves. And we know that this can come only as they are reconciled to God and to people through the gospel.

We share that gospel not just for our friends' sake, but for God's as well. For we know that, if they see him as he really is, they will be amazed and God will be honored. The following prayer, written hundreds of years ago during the Puritan era, has meant a great deal to me through the years.

Sovereign God, thy cause, not my own, engages my heart,
and I appeal to thee with the greatest freedom to
set up thy kingdom in every place where Satan
reigns.

Glorify thyself and I shall rejoice, for to bring honor to thy
name is my sole desire.

I adore thee that thou art God, and long that others should
know it, feel it, and rejoice in it.

O that all men might love and praise thee, that thou mightest
have all glory from the intelligent world!

Let sinners be brought to thee for thy dear name.

To the eye of reason everything respecting the conversion
of others is as dark as midnight, but thou canst accomplish great things; the cause is thine, and it is to
thy glory that men should be saved.

Lord, use me as thou wilt, do with me what thou wilt; but,
O, promote thy cause, let thy kingdom come, let thy
blessed interest be advanced in this world!

. . . While I live let me labor for thee to the utmost of my
strength, spending time profitably in this work, both
in health and in weakness.

It is thy cause and kingdom I long for, not my own.

O, answer thou my request.[5]

Renewing Everything

The other part of our mission—of equal importance to the
first—is renovation, in which we work to set our neighbors
free from whatever inhibits their enjoyment of God and his
world. All three levels of calling are involved in this: to know
and enjoy God (primary calling) is to love those who are in his

5. Arthur Bennett, ed., *The Valley of Vision: A Collection of Puritan Prayers
and Devotions* (Carlisle: The Banner of Truth Trust, 1975), 320–21.

image; I find myself (secondary calling) in large measure only as I express my gifts for the benefit of others; and sacrificial service to others (tertiary calling) is often simply necessary in our still-broken world.

By the power of the indwelling Holy Spirit we are to join the Second Adam in what he is doing. Wherever lies about the King flourish, we are called to speak against those lies and introduce people to the truth—one way of describing evangelism. But we go beyond this. Wherever lies of any sort flourish, whether this involves a parent doing his child's lab report or an executive lying about his company's profits or a friend spreading a false rumor about someone, we join our King in resisting and exposing them.

Wherever ugliness mars his handiwork in the natural order, we work to remove it—so that our neighbors and our children may better enjoy his beauty.

Wherever oppression or neglect keeps people from the full—or at least growing—discovery of their God-given wiring, we have an obligation to resist that oppression or neglect. Members of my church have volunteered for a number of summers to help paint the interiors of inner-city schools so that children return in the fall to environments that are a little more conducive to learning. One of our church leaders (a former university dean) has on occasion offered classes for inner-city kids on how to write a college application. My wife and I sponsor an inner-city child so that she can attend a very good private middle school in New York. In taking these sorts of actions members of our church family have increased the chances of young people to break free from some of the constraints imposed upon their freedom by their socio-economic circumstances. We are "doing for our neighbors what we would have our neighbors do for us" if the roles were reversed. And this is kingdom work—it advances shalom.

It's Not about Me

This point is so important that it bears repeating. If our pursuit of calling is all about ourselves—if it is principally about finding personal satisfaction, or even personal peace and joy—it will elude us. The call from the King is a call to his people to advance all that pleases him, whatever the cost.

This certainly involves learning to pray, engaging in personal evangelism, and building healthy relationships. But it is much bigger. We must engage, as God gives us opportunity, with everything, bringing every thought captive to the obedience of Christ.[6] N. T. Wright puts our call this way, emphasizing ecology, justice, and aesthetics:

> If the creation is to be renewed, not abandoned, and if that work has already begun in the resurrection of Jesus, it will not do simply to consign the present creation to acid rain and global warming and wait for Armageddon to destroy it altogether. Christians must be in the forefront of bringing, in the present time, signs and foretastes of God's eventual full healing to bear upon the created order in all its parts and at every level. If the world is to be put to rights, brought under the saving lordship of God's restorative justice, and if that work has already been unveiled prototypically in Jesus' death and resurrection, it will not do to concentrate on individual justification while allowing the wider issues of justice to go unaddressed. Christians must be in the forefront of bringing,

6. See 2 Cor. 10:5.

in the present time, signs and foretastes of God's healing justice to bear upon the world that is still full of corruption, injustice, oppression, division, suspicion, and war. And if the world is to attain its full beauty and dignity as God's liberated new creation, a beauty and dignity for which the present evidences of God's grandeur within creation are just a foretaste, it will not do to regard beauty, and its creation and preservation, as a pleasant but irrelevant optional extra within a world manipulated by science, exploited by technology, and bought and sold in the economic marketplace. Christians must be in the forefront of bringing, in the present time, signs and foretastes of God's fresh beauty to birth within the world, signs of hope for what the Spirit will yet do.[7]

A Certain Irony

There is a certain irony that a book about figuring out "my place in the scheme of things" should vigorously argue, "Stop thinking about yourself so much." But that is one of the great ironies of the kingdom of God. Life is not about me—it is not even about you. It is first about the King and his purposes, it is second about my neighbor, and it is only lastly about me. The way to self-discovery, self-satisfaction, and self-fulfillment is not, it turns out, via the self. I will know who I truly am only as I learn to live in the cosmos as it truly is and as it is soon to be, thanks to the Second Adam. And the cosmos is all about God—his glory, his character, and his purposes.

7. N. T. Wright, *The Letter to the Romans: Introduction, Commentary, and Reflections: Volume X, The New Interpreter's Bible* (Nashville: Abingdon Press, 2002), 605–6.

In other words, secondary calling must always be secondary. The discovery and expression of who I am will unfold only in the context of primary calling—the calling to know God and embrace his purposes. The best, and only, way to meet "me" is to meet God.

Questions
for Reflection and Discussion

1. Read aloud Cornelius Plantinga's imaginative description of a renovated world found in the chapter. Where do you see signs of the Second Adam's renewing work in our day? (List at least three items.)

2. Read again the following statement, found in the chapter:

   "We need to repent of our despair about the world. We need to change our thinking in the light of Jesus' work. Things may be changing slowly, but they are changing."

   Do you despair over the condition of the world? Why? Why not? Why, if you are a disciple of Jesus Christ, should you not despair?

3. Read through Wright's statement found near the end of the chapter. In what three areas of endeavor ought Christians to be "in the forefront"? Pick one and discuss

how you (or the group with which you are discussing this question) might be more fully engaged.

4. Alone or as a group, pray through the Puritan prayer found in the chapter. As you do, be specific about the people you know.

5. The final section of the chapter describes "a certain irony." What is that irony, and how have you seen it at work in your own experience?

5

Consummation
The View from the Top

I only began to hope when I ceased to be a materialist. . . . Material hopes cannot survive because they are material—that is, subject to corruption . . . [but] men [are] not made happy or unhappy, serene or unsettled by their circumstances whether physical or social or economic, but according to their sense of sharing a destiny which transcends their earthly circumstances, and consequent brotherliness between one another.

Malcolm Muggeridge*

Eye has not seen, nor ear heard, nor have entered into the heart of man the things which God has prepared for those who love him.

1 Corinthians 2:9 NKJV

* Ian Hunter, ed., *Things Past* (London: Collins, 1978), 36.

15

A Very Bright Future

n May 2004 I attended Yale's 303rd commencement exercises. Thousands of students, led by members of the faculty, all in academic regalia, solemnly and joyfully processed, college banners flying, to regal music by Holst, Berlioz, and others. Once everyone was in place, each group of candidates was presented to the president of the university by its appropriate dean with these words: "Mr. President, I present to you as candidates for the degree of _____ the following . . . " After each act of presentation the president of the university solemnly awarded the recommended degree and admitted the students to "all the rights and responsibilities" associated with their accomplishments—at which point that particular group of students exploded in jubilation.

The university then awarded honorary degrees to a remarkably broad range of individuals, including an Egyptologist, a researcher in breast cancer, a Kenyan environmentalist, and a novelist. Particularly moving was the tribute to Willie Mays, which included a video clip of his astonishing over-the-shoulder catch in the eighth inning of the first game of the 1954 World Series and spoke glowingly of his love for children and his work as a peacemaker. The massive assembly received Mr. Mays with a standing ovation.

Woven throughout the ceremony were remnants of Yale's beginnings as a theological institution. We acknowledged and welcomed God with the invocation, the benediction, and two hymns. One of the hymns, which has been regularly included in the festivities since 1718, includes these words:

> Thy praise, alone, O Lord, doth reign
> In Sion thine own hill:
> Their vows to thee they do maintain,
> And evermore fulfill . . .

A Glimpse of the Future

I have been to many commencements, but this particular one got hold of my imagination uniquely. It pictured our bright future. The hymns and prayers transported me to that great day when God will be fully honored. The sheer size and diversity of the gathering made me think of that day when God and his Messiah will be honored not just by a few of us, but by a "great multitude that no one could number, from every nation, from all tribes and peoples and languages."[1] The solemnity of the occasion reminded me that life is serious, that my life really does count. I am not traveling in pointless circles, but my life is on a trajectory: graduation is coming!

The honoring of so many different types of people and different types of accomplishments reminded me that Jesus has come to restore all human endeavor—that whatever I choose to do in life, therefore, is sacred. And the cheers that erupted from the students (not to mention their parents and friends) held before my imagination the astonishing hope that, because of Christ's lifework, my lifework may well be received with public praise, much to my joy and God's. I was reminded of the great promise implicit in the words of the master at the end of the parable of the talents: "Well done, good and faithful servant! You have been faithful with a few things; I will put you in charge of many things. Come and share your master's happiness."[2]

That Yale graduation pictured for me the fourth and final Big Idea that should frame our understanding and pursuit of calling in this life—the Idea of Consummation, whose meaning we will consider over the next six chapters. Here is a summary of its meaning.

The full discovery of who we are is certain, but still ahead, awaiting the return of the Second Adam. On that day we

1. Rev. 7:9 ESV.
2. Matt. 25:21, 23.

will become fully and freely ourselves, and fully integrated within ourselves. We will even love ourselves, not in the twisted way we do now, but with simple and humble delight in God's workmanship, happily sharing the cosmos with its rightful Owner. On that day love will triumph: every idolatrous pursuit of "calling" will be exposed and overthrown, every identity-squelching oppression will be removed, and every act of faithfulness will come to full flower and be honored. Our present sufferings will have their full meaning revealed and the pain of them will fade into obscurity. And all of this will happen because we will finally meet, face to face, the God who died and rose to make all things new, the God for whom we were made.

Can We Seriously Believe This?

The notion of such a radically transfigured future may strike you as fanciful—a throwback to an earlier, prescientific age. You no doubt have some friends who think it fanciful—or worse. And I suspect that, even if you say you believe in this vision, there are moments when you find it hard to buy. After all, life goes on more or less as it always has. Time and chance seem to rule. The skeptic in all of us whispers, "Get real! Don't be naïve." The pragmatist in all of us says, "Don't waste time and energy dreaming about what *may* be. Deal with what is *real*. Work at making *this* world a better place."

Such skepticism is understandable. But it is important to see that it arises from faith just as much as the Christian hope of consummation does. For we can no more disprove the notion of a transfigured future than we can prove it. There is,

196

in fact, compelling evidence, both historical and psychological, for the Christian hope.

The "status quo view" of the future makes little sense given the persistent belief in an afterlife that keeps springing up everywhere in human experience. It makes little sense, as well, of the place that "a better future" occupies in our imaginations a good part of the time—whether we are facing cancer or trying to build a government or simply looking forward to summer vacation. Shakespeare has said, "Hope springs eternal." We seem to be hard-wired for the future.

It is fashionable to argue that the hope of a transfigured future is little more than a coping mechanism we have acquired in the face of the unbearable fact of our inevitable extinction. The Bible argues differently. We look forward with hope because God has "set eternity in [our] hearts."[3] The resurrection of Jesus defines this hope and guarantees it for all who belong to him by faith. It declares that death has been undone, for Jesus has been re-embodied with a body that cannot perish (not simply resuscitated, only to die again).[4] His re-embodiment is the prelude to ours; Paul describes this as the "firstfruits" of the great harvest at the end of human history as we have known it. His triumph over death fills our present lives with meaning and guarantees that "our labor in the Lord is not in vain."[5]

3. Eccl. 3:11.

4. I cannot recommend strongly enough N. T. Wright's book *The Resurrection of the Son of God* (Minneapolis: Fortress Press, 2003). It brilliantly, comprehensively, and convincingly sets forth the evidence for and the meaning of the resurrection of Jesus.

5. 1 Cor. 15:20, 58.

Something to Look Forward To

When I was a teenager, struggling to be a disciple of Jesus in the midst of the usual temptations, there was a certain kind of sermon I could never resonate with. It was the "Come quickly, Lord Jesus!" sermon. I just could not see how anybody—certainly anybody my age—could get excited about that idea. I was young and had so much to experience. I wanted to go to college. I wanted to travel. I wanted to fall in love, get married, enjoy legitimate sex, and have children. The prospect of a perfect and endless eternity with nothing but harp lessons and clouds had no appeal.

I later changed my mind when I discovered that I had been poorly taught about heaven. C. S. Lewis and others helped me to see that the final state will not be disembodied, but re-embodied, not less diverse but more diverse, than the present state. How could the God who gave us sex, Michael Jordan, Rembrandt, and the Grand Canyon—all in our present fallen world—give us something less interesting in the next?!

With that vision of greater fullness came a peace of mind about the limitations of my experience and the limitations in my own present makeup. To be specific about one particular issue that preoccupied me as a teenager, I began to see that whatever it was about sex that drew my attention, it must be a distant echo of something far more satisfying that awaits us when we, as the bride of Christ, meet our Bridegroom face to face. The embrace that will follow that encounter, and what unfolds beyond that, are impossible to imagine, but the satisfaction, delight, and richness of those things will dwarf the very best that our present experience can offer.

What will sports be like in glory? How about scientific research? How about food? How about painting and music and swimming and housing (every room with a view!)? Who knows? But somehow love, creativity, beauty, and pleasure will all be intertwined, and all growing, for the person at the center of glory will be the Creator and Giver of every good and perfect gift—and he is infinite.

Many things now stand in the way of the full and satisfying expression of our God-given gifts and motivations. Much in our fallen world inhibits our development as people. We rightly care for people in need (the poor, our children, aging parents), but this can often be at enormous cost in time and energy—resources that might otherwise be spent discovering and developing our particular gifts. Inner struggles can paralyze us. Oppressive parents, friends, or governments shut down much of our creative effort. But that is OK. A better and infinitely more satisfying day is coming just around the corner. We can afford to be patient.

Questions
for Reflection and Discussion

1. Think again of the description of the commencement ceremony at the beginning of the chapter. Discuss or reflect on two interesting and comforting ways that that event points toward the experience of heaven.

2. Does the notion of heaven bore you? If so, why? If not, why not? What excites you about heaven?

3. What losses, inner weaknesses, or limiting circumstances have frustrated your development as a person? How does the promise of the consummation help you to cope with those losses, inner weaknesses, or limiting circumstances?

4. Read the following statement from the chapter:

    I began to see that whatever it was about sex that drew my attention, it must be a distant echo of something far more satisfying that awaits us when we, as the bride of Christ, meet our Bridegroom face to face. The embrace that will follow that encounter, and what unfolds beyond that, are impossible to imagine, but the satisfaction, delight, and richness of those things will dwarf the very best that our present experience can offer.

What are the things about sex that make it so powerful in our lives, and how might those things come to more satisfying expression in the new heavens and the new earth?

Trust in the Lord and do good.

Psalm 37:3

16

Freedom to Commit

D ale Davis tells a story about the nineteenth-century
Princeton theologian B. B. Warfield:

The works of . . . Warfield . . . are still known and read in
the evangelical church today. What is not so well-known
is the tale of his marriage. Warfield was pursuing studies in
Leipzig, Germany, in 1876–77. This time also doubled as
his honeymoon with his wife Annie. They were on a walking tour in the Harz Mountains when they were caught in a
terrific thunderstorm. The experience was such a shock to

Annie that she never fully recovered, becoming more or less an invalid for life. Warfield only left her for seminary duties, but never for more than two hours at a time. His world was almost entirely limited to Princeton and to the care of his wife. For thirty-nine years. One of his students noted that when he saw the Warfields out walking together "the gentleness of his manner was striking proof of the loving care with which he surrounded her." For thirty-nine years.[1]

Could we make with such evident grace the choices that Warfield made for four decades? Do we want to risk marrying when we cannot predict how healthy our spouse will be in the years ahead? These are fair questions that haunt young people in our day—even those young people who go to church and say that they believe in the Christian story.

Functional Secularists

The reason they haunt us is that many of us, regardless of what we say we believe, are functionally secular. We have bought the line that this is the only life. If we don't find the perfect mate, and are stuck for life with someone who is less than perfect, then we will have ultimately missed out.

Our difficulties making relational commitments are made worse by our mobility and the over-choice arising from it. In New York, for example, so many interesting and attractive people "cycle through" that it is often difficult to commit to just one. Why should I risk marrying Sally when Susie or Jane (whom I see every day at work, or who may move here next week from some other part of the country) may prove

1. Dale Ralph Davis, *2 Samuel: Out of Every Adversity* (Ross-shire, Great Britain: Christian Focus Publications, 2001), 102.

to be more interesting in certain ways, or when Sally might become chronically sick? If I make the wrong choice, my life will be ruined.

Without commitment—whether to a relationship or to a career path—there can be no growth. Without commitment, in other words, calling (especially the discovery of our God-given wiring) languishes. But we are afraid to commit because we are desperate to keep our options open. And we are desperate to keep our options open because, deep down, we believe that this is the only life—or at least the only life in which fun and interesting things happen.

Freedom from Fear of Failure

What happens when we make a significant career choice and then experience failure, or the likelihood of it? When I was forty-nine years old I left a stable suburban parish and moved to New York City to plant a church. There were many times, especially during the first three years, when I would look at my wife and say, "What was I thinking when I agreed to do this?" We had sold our house and left our good friends behind. I was at the season of life where failure in this new venture could not be easily absorbed by moving on to another church situation. Finding available and affordable rental space for worship was close to impossible. (I remember the moment when one more in a long series of glitches threatened to shut down lease negotiations for the only available worship space in our part of town: I collapsed on the floor of my apartment, crying, "Lord, I cannot take this any longer!") Leaders came and went with mind-blurring rapidity—so much so that it can easily be said that I planted the same church at least three times.

During those very trying first years well-wishers would try to console me by saying, "It certainly is reassuring, isn't it, that God called you to New York to do this work." My response (thought, even if unspoken) was this: "I am confident that Jesus Christ is going to build his church in this part of New York, and I am reasonably sure that Jesus has called me to be a minister. But what I have no sure word about is that the Lord Jesus has decided to use *me*, and my particular (and fallible) church planting vision, to do his thing in this part of New York." There were many times when circumstances forced me to face squarely the possibility that all the money I had raised and all the work I had done would simply disappear down the drain. That remains a possibility as I write these words.

Let me tell you another story. I have a friend who is a surgeon. At least fifteen years ago he decided to move his wife and his three children to Bangladesh where he took charge of a mission clinic and hospital in a rural area of the country. He did this as a long-term career move, despite the fears and objections of his broader family. He did it knowing that the decision meant almost certain career suicide back in this country. He did it knowing that the government and people where he was going could be very hostile to Christian presence (when I visited him, I preached in a church near the clinic that had no roof because the local populace had recently burned it, along with a number of nearby Christian homes). He made the move knowing that the health care there was substandard, exposing him and his family to significant health risks: the likelihood of career-ending disease was, in other words, very great.

It is easy in such situations to become fearful. And what often lies back of such fear is an even deeper one—that the career decision will have turned out to be a "mistake." It is bad enough to seal off a number of career options by committing to one particular path. But it is much worse, having abandoned a host of other possibilities, to fail in the one you have chosen. It is much safer not to risk any choice at all.

Freedom from Fear of a Wasted Life

But we do not have to play it safe—nor should we. For we are children of the consummation. Failure in a chosen career path can be very hard—but it is never "the end" for someone who firmly believes that this is not the only life. Forty years (or even sixty) in a difficult relationship may seem a long time—but they are a blip on the screen of eternity. It is true that every time we make a significant choice we diminish our options in life. But diminished options now do not mean diminished options forever.

Nor do failed careers or long and arduous relationships mean that our lives have been wasted. For the hope of consummation means much more than that life goes on beyond the grave. It means that all things—even failures and relational pain—belong to a God-driven trajectory that will turn into something immensely good in us:

Consider it pure joy, my brothers, whenever you face trials of many kinds, because you know that the testing of your faith develops perseverance. Perseverance must finish its work so that you may be mature and complete, not lacking anything.[2]

James (the writer of these words) is not asking us to pretend that bad things are good. But he is telling us that there is deep cause for joy even in the hardest things, for the God of the consummation will work through them, refining our faith, if we persevere, so as to make us full and mature people.

This is true, we must remember, regardless of the source of the trial—whether it arises from persecution, from the brokenness of life in general, or even from our own sin. Paul reminds us that "all things [not just "some things"] work together for good to them that love God, to them who are the called according to his purpose."[3] Sometimes we can see the good things that God is up to—as when a collapsed career restores a parent to his or her children, or a failed relationship exposes deep-seated selfishness and leads to important changes. But many times, especially when there is no obvious lesson to be learned, we have to wait to figure things out. We wait, however, with hope, for we are children of the consummation.

We Don't Need It All Now

People in their twenties and thirties frequently ask me for advice on what to do with their lives. They may have no solid career plans, they may be struggling with whether to change from one career to another, or they may be struggling over their motives. Beneath the surface they are often

2. James 1:2–4.
3. Rom. 8:28 KJV.

afraid—afraid that time is running out, afraid that they will miss out on a fulfilling life, afraid that they will never discover who they are, afraid that God will punish them for their mixed motives.

I try to be practical—to talk about what they love to do, about what opportunities now exist, about training and educational opportunities. But I also try to get them to relax about the big picture and decide on whatever at the moment makes the most sense. I remind them that God never runs out of time and is far more patient than we are at unpacking who we are. I remind them that they are free to choose a career path that doesn't look like a perfect fit, because whatever they lose out on in this life will be more than made up for in the next. I remind them that it is important to be aware of their mixed motives, but not to be paralyzed by them. Our motives will never be completely pure, and Jesus died to cover that problem so that we could get on with our lives.

I remind them as well that they do not have to be afraid of failure—not because failure will never happen, but because God folds failure into his good agenda for us. This fact remains true, I remind them, even when failure arises not simply from their circumstances or limits, but also from their selfishness and idolatry. They must choose thoughtfully and with humility. But they can, and should, choose.

I also look for the "gotta have it all now" syndrome and expose it if I see it. What drives both indecision and overcommitment is the desperate and wrong-headed longing to cram as many experiences and achievements as possible into one's life. (The over-committed obviously are doing this—but the indecisive may be doing it as well, because their indecision is driven in part by the fear of missing out on "x" if they choose "y.") I urge those I speak with to let go of certain things and to do so knowing that, if they die without ever having sailed in a tall ship or having visited Alaska, it's OK. There will be enough time in glory to do those things.

I myself plan to build and captain my own sailing yacht— and then learn to play the organ.

Questions
for Reflection and Discussion

1. What does it mean to be "functionally secular"? Where do you see evidence of functional secularism in your own behavior?

2. How does being functionally secular show up in both overcommitment and indecision?

3. Does fear of failure, in either career or in relationships, control your decision-making in any way? If so, how and why?

4. Do you fear that God will punish you if you make a career decision with mixed motives? Should you fear this? Why? Why not?

5. Why do we need not fear that we will have a wasted life if we make imperfect choices, or if difficult circumstances undermine our choices?

There are no *ordinary* people. You have never talked to a mere mortal. Nations, cultures, arts, civilisations—these are mortal, and their life is to ours as the life of a gnat. But it is immortals whom we joke with, work with, marry, snub, and exploit— immortal horrors or everlasting splendours.

C. S. Lewis, *The Weight of Glory*

17

Bringing People
with Us

W e have already met Ying, the talented young artist who turned her music for a time into a God
substitute. She goes on in her story to tell of the
transforming impact of people in her life:

But God did not stop pursuing me in His love. He used people,
mainly, to show me that what I thirsted for in my musical
pursuits could only be found in relationship, and relationship
based on Christ. A Christian classmate at Juilliard, whom I had

scoffed at for a long while for being deficient in her devotion to Art, unbeknownst to me, started praying that we would have fellowship together. This friendship became a source of solace to me, while the ties I had formed with others, based on achievement and worldly accomplishment, were showing themselves to be tenuous, self-serving, and disappointing.

Healed through the love of people, Ying started to become a healer herself, drawing musical friends into the community of Jesus. As she came to realize that her music community included many lonely, searching young musicians, she came up with a plan to connect many of them to the church community. She and other musicians created the Elbereth Chamber Music Series, offering a series of free concerts in our church. Musicians, the church body, and the wider community were all introduced to one another.

You Can't Take It with You: But You Can Take People

Lee Iacocca, former CEO of Chrysler, once said that he couldn't imagine anyone saying on his deathbed, "I wish I had spent more time at the office."

All we can bring with us past the grave is other people. If we are "people of the consummation," we will therefore hold more tightly to people than to careers or experiences or feelings.

The married ones among us will take the time and expend the necessary energy to welcome each other properly. We will let go of our idolatrous fantasies about the perfect marriage and learn to love the actual person we happen to be married to, even (and especially) when it costs us. Mike Mason describes marriage's particular intrusiveness vividly:

A marriage, or a marriage partner, may be compared to a great tree growing right up through the center of one's living room. It is something that is just there, and it is huge, and everything has been built around it, and wherever one happens to be going—to the fridge, to bed, to the bathroom, to the front door—the tree has to be taken into account. It cannot be gone through; it must be respectfully gone around. It is somehow bigger and stronger than oneself. True, it could be chopped down, but not without tearing the house apart. And certainly it is beautiful, unique, exotic: but also, let's face it, it is at times an enormous inconvenience.[1]

The parents among us will pay our parental dues: late nights, early mornings, missed golf outings, missed job opportunities, important conversations at inconvenient times. The employees and employers will respect the people we work with and for, even (and especially) the ones who are difficult or at the bottom of the employment ladder. The students among us will not treat our teachers as mere means to the end of the grade or degree that we want; instead we will honor and pray for them. We will remember that every person we meet—bureaucrats, politicians, sanitation workers, the beautiful and the ugly, celebrities and low-lifes, people we like and people we don't like—every one of these is progressing (whether he admits it or not) toward the ultimate "commencement." C. S. Lewis writes:

> It may be possible for each to think too much of his own potential glory hereafter; it is hardly possible for him to think too often or too deeply about that of his neighbour. . . . It is

1. John Mason, *The Mystery of Marriage* (Portland: Multnomah Press, 1985), 31.

a serious thing to live in a society of possible gods and god-desses, to remember that the dullest and most uninteresting person you can talk to may one day be a creature which, if you saw it now, you would be strongly tempted to worship, or else a horror and a corruption such as you now meet, if at all, only in a nightmare. All day long we are, in some degree, helping each other to one or other of these destinations. . . . There are no *ordinary* people. You have never talked to a mere mortal. Nations, cultures, arts, civilisations—these are mortal, and their life is to ours as the life of a gnat. But it is immortals whom we joke with, work with, marry, snub, and exploit—im-mortal horrors or everlasting splendours.[2]

To remember the consummation is to remember people. It is to see and value and long for people in the light of that consummation.

A Satisfying Commencement

Imagine a university commencement in which you are the sole participant: noble architecture, colorful regalia, flying banners, stirring music, and you, all by yourself, conferring and receiving degrees. What loneliness. What emptiness. To pursue self-discovery and self-fulfillment while snubbing people is to prepare for just such a commencement.

We can put things a happier way. If we leave the award-ing of our degrees—the defining of our lives—in the hands of the coming King, and give our attention to people, then commencement will be worth attending, and full of happy surprises. This applies to *every* human encounter, but espe-

2. C. S. Lewis, *The Weight of Glory* (New York: Macmillan, 1949), 18–19.

cially to our encounters with those who are outside the gospel and its benefits. We will find no needy people in glory, nor will we find any nonbelievers. If we are ever to extend the love and truth of the coming King to such folks, now is the time.

Questions
for Reflection and Discussion

1. Read again the statement by C. S. Lewis at the head of the chapter. Identify a friend or family member whom you are now treating as a "mere mortal." How might you improve your behavior?

2. In what ways do you make work more important than people? Be specific (about your behavior in marriage, as a parent, at work, or as a student).

3. Discuss or reflect on the truth and challenge of the following statement:

   No spouse is married to marriage; he or she is married to a particular person and must learn to love that particular person.

4. To say that we must put people first does not mean that we should simply allow them to control our lives. Think of a situation in your life in which there is a

legitimate tension between people and work. How are you addressing that tension? If you are in a group, seek advice from one another on how to make a priority of people without allowing people to run your lives.

Listen, I tell you a mystery: We will not all sleep, but we shall all be changed—in a moment, in the twinkling of an eye, at the last trumpet. For the trumpet will sound, the dead will be raised imperishable, and we will be changed. For the perishable must clothe itself with the imperishable, and the mortal with immortality. When the perishable has been clothed with the imperishable, and the mortal with immortality, then the saying that is written will come true: "Death has been swallowed up in victory." "Where, O death, is your victory? Where, O death, is your sting?" The sting of death is sin, and the power of sin is the law. But thanks be to God! He gives us the victory through our Lord Jesus Christ. Therefore, my dear brothers, stand firm. Let nothing move you. Always give yourselves fully to the work of the Lord, because you know that your labor in the Lord is not in vain.

1 Corinthians 15:51–58

18

A Reason to Work Hard

My first job after college was as a hospital house-keeping manager. After six months of training I was sent to a "start-up" in Albany. My assignment was to retrain the existing staff in my company's materials, techniques, and standards. Olga (I have forgotten her real name) was one of the finest housekeepers in the hospital, hard working and meticulous. Her rooms were always spotless, the beds perfectly made, everything as it should be—and you could see that she took pride in her work. The only problem was that she took more time per room than my company could afford. What added to the difficulty was that she was a Romanian immigrant who spoke little English.

I let things continue status quo for a while. But I knew that I had to speak with Olga eventually. When I did, what happened broke my heart. I wanted her to know how deeply I appreciated her attitude and hard work—but that she did not actually need to be quite so thorough. All she seemed to hear me say was that I was displeased with her work and wanted her to work harder. She ended up quitting in tears.

I had a friend in college who spent his summers working in a steel mill. He was a motivated laborer. One day one of the regulars at the plant pulled him aside and warned him with a story. He told him about a foreman who had pushed the men harder than they wanted to be pushed—so much so that one of them loaded gunpowder into the base of his ashtray. One day he blew three of his fingers off while smoking a cigar during lunch break.

Many things stand in the way of the satisfaction of putting in a good day's work that we can be proud of. Sometimes it is the requirements of management, as with Olga. Sometimes it is pressure from fellow workers (which may or may not have reasonable cause), as with my college friend. This can be very frustrating, and doesn't always have easy solutions. My college friend would have risked the ire of (and perhaps injury from) his fellow workers if he had persisted in his work ethic. Olga's high standards could not easily be matched with the demands of my company's contract with the hospital.

Hope in the Broken Workplace

No lifework—no job, no family situation, no academic or artistic or athletic undertaking—is without its deep flaws. The Fall, as we have noted already, permeates everything in life. But hope permeates everything as well. Notice how comprehensive that hope is, according to the apostle Paul:

> And he made known to us the mystery of his will according to his good pleasure, which he purposed in Christ, to be put into effect when the times will have reached their fulfillment—to bring *all things* in heaven and on earth together under one head, even Christ. . . . [God] raised him from the dead and seated him at his right hand in the heavenly realms, far above all rule and authority, power and dominion, and every title that can be given, not only in the present age but in the one to come.[1]

There is absolutely nothing in life, including work, that Jesus will not have fixed by the time his plan is fully realized. This is so because he is in charge of everything.

I caught a glimpse of the bright future of work when my church helped build a Habitat for Humanity house for a poor family. The home went up with astonishing speed, the site humming with the happy labor of scores of people of all ages and races. Of particular pleasure throughout the project was meeting the family, who joined us as the work

1. Eph. 1:9–10, 20–21.

progressed. Little in my life has matched the satisfaction I felt the morning we dedicated the house and the new inhabitants welcomed the crew inside for a party. Here was work that was productive, purposeful, joyful, satisfying, in community with others—a little picture of heaven's economy at work.

Imagine work situations unplagued by miscommunication, business transactions unsullied by greed, compensation that is always fair and appropriate, people who are always suitably placed and happy with their placement. Imagine workers who are always diligent and productive, never joyless or driven. Imagine cooperating on a project without competition spoiling either the relationships or the work. Imagine an office environment completely free from fear and posturing. Dreaming more broadly, picture soccer matches without fouls, diplomacy without duplicity, and research without vested interest. These sorts of realities—or better—are what Jesus has in store. And they are what he intends us to be working toward now, since his reign has already begun.

Concerts in Heaven

I have wondered what piano playing will be like after we "graduate" from this broken world. Certainly, everyone who wants to play the piano will be able to. There will always be enough pianos and affordable teachers around; neither race nor poverty will inhibit anyone; arthritis won't be an issue; neither will fear. Life at the keyboard will become a life-expanding joy, not a lonely obsession that competes with love. In that new world every pianist will finally discover, enjoy, and share his or her own particular (and no doubt evolving) style, thereby making the "new piano world" breathtakingly rich and beautiful—like New York, only infinitely more so. For with the richness and self-discovery will also come the final obliteration of selfishness. Every artist's offering will be made in simplicity, out of simple childlike love for the heavenly Giver and for his or her hearers.

Let's consider the practical help that this vision gives in our still-fallen world. Today's hard-working Christian artist who holds tightly to the vision finds strength to fight against laziness, frustration, fear, and envy—attitudes that tend to cripple the creative enterprise. She can play, for example, before a hostile audience if she is convinced that one day all hostile audiences will cease. She can pick up after a terrible concert or lesson and try again, knowing that she does not need to make her mark in this life and that the Lord will commend in the end every faithful effort she makes—even if no one else does. She can enter a competition with less apprehension when she recalls that competitions in glory (if there are any) will be celebrations of diversity rather than occasions for triumph at someone else's expense. She can work hard, even if she is not the best, knowing that in glory variations in ability will not be the basis upon which we evaluate each other. And she can take some of the time she might spend practicing to be with family, friends, and the church community—knowing that she will have eternity to hone her keyboard skills.

A Reason to Keep at It

What I have just said applies not simply to musicians. It would have helped Olga, the Romanian hospital housekeeper, to trust that God noted all her hard work, even if her manager didn't seem to, and that God would one day commend her for it. It would have helped my friend in the steel mill to know that his frustration over being obliged to work less diligently was noted by the God who will one day free us all to work to our potential. It would have helped him to know, as well, that the pressure he felt to slow down was in part the legitimate reaction by the labor force to managerial oppression in the past, and therefore a sign pointing to the great day when oppression will no longer be found anywhere in the marketplace. It would have made him patient.

The hope of glory fights off all the things that keep us from working steadily and giving our best to what we do—even when our best is constrained. That hope fights off discouragement, laziness, cynicism, envy, and fear in all of us: believing students, athletes, store clerks, attorneys, police officers, or parents. The believer, whatever he is doing, can risk hard work. Though he will take care not to turn work into a substitute god, he can nevertheless press forward toward high moral, intellectual, and aesthetic achievement. He can do so in the face of a barrage of resistance and disappointment because he sees beyond the present horizon. He sees a place where hard work, sacrificial love, and beautiful craftsmanship are all honored.

We must not (yet) expect perfect work environments, satisfying results, or steady encouragement for what we labor over. Nevertheless we can and should work in hope—doing the little things as well as the big things (the things bosses and others see and the things they don't see) with diligence; with an eye for what is right, beautiful, and good; and with love driving us. For the Lord of the great consummation sees everything, and our labor is not in vain in him.[2]

2. 1 Cor. 15:58.

Questions
for Reflection and Discussion

1. What keeps you from working hard and joyfully at whatever you have been given to do? Why does this inhibit you?

2. What would your present work environment look like if it were free from the things that tend to inhibit work in the way God intended it? What is one thing you could do to make things better?

3. Discuss together the following statement, found at the end of the chapter. Do you find it helpful or unrealistic?

   The believer, whatever he is doing, can risk hard work. Though he will take care not to turn work into a substitute god, he can nevertheless press forward toward high moral, intellectual, and aesthetic achievement. He can do so in the face of a barrage of resistance and disappointment because he sees beyond the present horizon. He sees a place where

hard work, sacrificial love, and beautiful craftsman-
ship are all honored.

4. Discuss together the following statement, also found at the end of the chapter. What one little thing and one big thing are calling for your diligence at the moment?

We must not (yet) expect perfect work environments, satisfying results, or steady encouragement for what we labor over. Nevertheless we can and should work in hope—doing the little things as well as the big things (the things bosses and others see and the things they don't see) with diligence; with an eye for what is right, beautiful, and good; and with love driving us. For the Lord of the great consumma- tion sees everything, and our labor is not in vain in him.

We know that the whole creation has been groaning as in the pains of childbirth right up to the present time. Not only so, but we ourselves, who have the firstfruits of the Spirit, groan inwardly as we wait eagerly for our adoption as sons, the redemption of our bodies. For in this hope we were saved. But hope that is seen is no hope at all. Who hopes for what he already has? But if we hope for what we do not yet have, we wait for it patiently.

Romans 8:22–25

19

An Invitation
to Patience

very so often we find ourselves completely "in the zone"—completely in sync with our God-given "wiring." Os Guinness describes such a moment in the life of a great jazz musician:

> After one utterly extraordinary rendition of "A Love Supreme," [John] Coltrane stepped off the stage, put down his saxophone, and said simply, "Nunc Dimittis." Coltrane felt he could never play the piece more perfectly. If his whole life had been lived for that passionate thirty-two minute jazz prayer, it would have been worth it. He was ready to go.[1]

1. Os Guinness, *The Call* (Nashville: Word Publishing, 1998), 45. "Nunc

Perhaps you have experienced this sort of thing, either alone or with a group of people.

My freshman year at Harvard, our football team met Yale for the final game of the season—both teams undefeated. Yale was heavily favored, boasting two remarkable players who went on to play professionally. As expected, Yale moved to a comfortable lead, so that with less than three minutes remaining the score was 29–13.

And then something happened. Harvard entered "the zone." With 2:40 left in the game Harvard began a drive that ended in a touchdown. They made the two-point conversion, and then did an onside kick—which they recovered. What followed was another drive that resulted in a touchdown as the clock ran out. People were so worked up that they poured onto the field even before Harvard could set up for the extra points. After the field was cleared, play resumed as people on both sides held their breath. A mad scramble in the backfield issued in a completed pass to the end zone, and the fans went wild. As we left the stadium, hawkers from the school newspaper greeted us with a "hot-off-the-press" broadside, crowing "Harvard Beats Yale: 29-29." Though logically imprecise (it was a tie), it captured the mood perfectly.

This was not, of course, a happy time for Yale. But for folks on the other side it was a once-in-a-lifetime moment—a moment in which everything seemed to converge in a happy direction. Everything simply flowed—a flow all the more remarkable because no one had expected it.

---

dimittis" is the Latin for "Now dismiss"—words spoken by the elderly prophet Simeon when he saw the baby Jesus in the temple. His full statement was, "Sovereign Lord, as you have promised, you now dismiss your servant [i.e., let me die] in peace. For my eyes have seen your salvation" (Luke 2:29–30).

Windows on Eternity

Such moments are indescribably satisfying. For Coltrane it was as if he had found the center of things; his life overflowed with love and meaning. One gets the impression that he felt as though he could go on forever in this state and never be bored, for somehow he would always be growing. For the Harvard team and fans it wasn't quite so dramatic, perhaps. Nevertheless that day will never be forgotten—certainly not in this fan's imagination—because there was something so right and joyous and full, even inevitable, about it.

I am convinced that such moments are sneak previews on the consummation, the future "breaking in" on the present. I experienced this another time in a concert performance of Mozart's *Requiem*. The concert began with a fascinating lecture by professor and Mozart scholar Robert Levin, in which he explained the variations between his recent completion of the *Requiem* and the traditional one by Sussmeier. (Mozart died before he was able to complete it.) We then settled in for an outstanding performance of the work. When the piece ended something happened that I had never before experienced in a concert hall. Dead silence stretched far beyond the last echoes of the final chord. After what seemed an interminable period, the house suddenly went wild.

My assessment of that strange experience is that, thanks to the combination of the transcendent text (the worldview explicit in the *Requiem* is God-centered and eternal), the excellent performance, and the astounding power and beauty of the composition, those assembled were carried (perhaps despite themselves) into the presence of the One who made the event possible. Believer and nonbeliever alike somehow knew that it would have been trite simply to applaud—simply to thank those who had just performed. Something (some One) bigger needed to be acknowledged. In the end, not knowing quite whom to thank, we fell back on convention and cheered the performers.

Closing Windows

The frustrating thing about these "break-ins" is that they do not last. For me, the effect of that concert began to fade within minutes of the final bars. Coltrane didn't suddenly blast off to heaven when he left the stage. And the wonder of that football game in the fall of 1968 has long since faded.

The great danger for us, living this side of the great consummation, is that we will obsess about holding on to, or recapturing, such moments. We will re-create all the details of last year's great family holiday in order to try to recapture, this year, the wonderful harmony we enjoyed then. We will drill our football team into the ground or rehearse our violins until our fingers bleed in the hopes of recapturing the experience of last year's great season or of last year's wonderful concert.

Such obsessions are doomed; heavenly "break-ins" are gifts of God—we can at best only parody them. And they divert us from our present task. God never commands, "Make eternity happen now! Realize your full potential now!" Instead he says, "Love me with all your heart and love your neighbor as yourself: Do *that* now, and I'll take care of the future." This does not mean that we cease to work hard and diligently; it means only that we let go of the need (or demand) to experience God in some breathtaking way in our work or as a result of it.

Think again of George Bailey in the film "It's a Wonderful Life." Repeatedly, great opportunities to get out of town, to improve his mind, and to discover the world come and go, all because love beckons him to stay. His father dies on the eve of his departure for college, so he postpones his plans in order to run the family banking business, and in the end never goes. The day he and his wife marry and are scheduled to leave on their honeymoon, there is a run on the bank, and they give all their vacation cash away to stem the tide of the panic and save his clients from the greedy Mr. Potter.

This is how we should live—steadily doing what we must. Our job is not to clamor after those things that only God can give; it is to leave the "big picture" in God's hands and press on with whatever requires our obedience today. God will break in if and when he chooses (he does this for George Bailey at the end of the film). Our job is to be found working steadily at our posts, however insignificant that post may seem to be, when Christ comes.

The certainty of the great consummation gives us an enormous incentive to hang in there, even when the experience of it eludes us. At the climax of *It's a Wonderful Life*, George Bailey cries out in despair, "I wish I had never been born." What follows, kindness of the angel Clarence, is a vision of what Bedford Falls would be like if George's wish were granted. He begins to realize that every good decision he had ever made, every kindness, every sacrifice, was in fact weighty with significance.

So it is with us. Every act of trust-driven obedience, however obscure, is noted. Every choice to let go of the glory, every decision to wait for fulfillment so that I can care for somebody else, is weighty with meaning. In ways that I can never imagine, but will one day see, every such choice shifts the flow of history and increases God's own delight. "Whoever finds his life," said Jesus, "will lose it, and whoever loses his life for my sake will find it."[2]

2. Matt. 10:39.

Questions
for Reflection and Discussion

1. Recall a "break-in" experience. What happened? How have you sought (if you have) to recapture that moment?

2. Watch the film "It's a Wonderful Life" with some friends and discuss its message. How does George Bailey's life illustrate the proper alternative to living for (or out of) a "break-in" experience? In what ways have you made "George Bailey-like" choices?

3. Discuss the following statement, found at the end of the chapter. Recall an occasion of "trust-driven obedience" or delayed gratification in your life or someone else's. Try to note how those choices have changed things in some way for the better.

   Every act of trust-driven obedience, however obscure, is noted. Every choice to let go of the glory, every decision to wait for fulfillment so that I can care for somebody else, is weighty with meaning. In ways that I can never imagine, but will one day see, every such choice shifts the flow of history and increases God's own delight. "Whoever finds his life," said Jesus, "will lose it, and whoever loses his life for my sake will find it."

4. Pray over a number of your acts of "trust-driven obedience," thanking God for his work through them, asking for patience in the waiting time.

You make known to me the path of life; in your presence there is fullness of joy; at your right hand are pleasures forevermore.

Psalm 16:11 ESV

20

Enjoying God Now

The very heart of the great consummation is God. God will one day come to judge and to rule over the earth. We will know him so fully that knowledge of him will "fill the earth as the waters cover the sea." He will never depart, but will shine like a sun that never sets.[1] We

1. See Ps. 96:13; Isa. 11:9; and Rev. 22:5.

will survive that sun—his appearing will be a delight rather than a terror—because he has already borne our sins away by his infinite and undeserved sufferings on our behalf. But we will do more than survive this sun. We will see him, and something about that sight will change us beyond hope and imagining:

> How great is the love the Father has lavished on us, that we should be called children of God! And that is what we are! The reason the world does not know us is that it did not know him. Dear friends, now we are children of God, and what we will be has not yet been made known. But we know that when he appears, we shall be like him, for we shall see him as he is.[2]

Self-discovery will blossom in the midst of God-discovery as a flower opens under the sun.[3]

Getting Ready

How do we get ready for that great day? Certainly we must surrender to and trust in God's Messiah Jesus, without whose

---

2. 1 John 3:1–2.

3. Calvin writes of the disturbing self-discoveries that come from seeing God: "If in broad daylight we either look down upon the ground or survey whatever meets our view round about, we seem to ourselves endowed with the strongest and keenest sight; yet when we look up to the sun and gaze straight at it, that power of sight which was particularly strong on earth is at once blunted and confused by a great brilliance and thus we are compelled to admit that our keenness in looking upon things earthly is sheer dullness when it comes to the sun. So it happens when estimating our spiritual goods" (*Institutes of the Christian Religion*, Book 1, Ch. I.2). Under the gospel, the infinite glory of God will no doubt still overwhelm us—but it will draw us upward out of sin into joy and satisfaction rather than crushing us.

incarnation, obedience, suffering, and death (all undertaken in our place) we could never survive God's appearing.[4] But that is not enough. In fact it is not the heart of things, for coming under the protection of the Messiah has a purpose beyond it. We get ready for glory by learning to enjoy God now. Why? Because that is what life, now and forever, is fundamentally about: "The chief end of man is to glorify God and to enjoy him forever."[5]

We enjoy God certainly in public worship. Gathering with other "enjoyers" can have a remarkable effect on our ability to enjoy him—even if they sing flat and don't like the same liturgy or style of music that we like. Worship is not always easy or comfortable or familiar. It is an acquired taste, like learning to appreciate good wine. It takes work, especially if we have been raised on other, lesser, enjoyments—some of which we may have to unlearn completely. But it is absolutely necessary if we are going to begin to enjoy God.

More Than Public Worship

But public worship is not the only setting in which we learn to enjoy God. He is the Giver of "every good and perfect gift," and our wonder at his greatness and grace expands as we learn to enjoy him in all life's enjoyments—in the screeching violins of our children's spring concerts, in the first warm breeze of spring, in an exciting ballgame, in a tasty mouthful

4. See Mal. 3:1–2: "The Lord you are seeking will come to his temple . . . But who can endure the day of his coming? Who can stand when he appears?"
5. The Westminster Shorter Catechism, Question 1 (The Publications Committee of the Free Presbyterian Church of Scotland, 1976 Edition, 287).

of well-prepared food, in the satisfaction of terribly prepared food when we are famished or when another has prepared it in love, in the joy of learning a skill or making a fresh discovery in science or learning something new about God's world in the presence of its Maker.

Enjoying God can even happen in the rebuke of a friend or a child. I remember the first time that my teenage son took me aside to challenge me about speaking harshly to his mother. At first I was taken aback, and then I rejoiced to see God's hand at work in making a brother out of a son.

We need to learn to live with God 24/7, to enjoy life with him. I am not talking about something super-spiritual here. Certainly we may have long times of deep and serious prayer, mission trips, times of weeping in confession and repentance. But we can also experience this other, fuller thing, the best analogy to which is a good friendship. In a bad friendship we avoid each other, hide things from each other, and perform for each other. But in a good friendship, we enjoy each other: we laugh together, do things together, tell silly jokes, share the things that interest us, go places together—we even waste time together. God isn't a "pal," if by that term we mean someone we can take advantage of or be rude to. But he calls himself our friend,[6] and by so doing invites us into that sort of relationship with him.

Certainly "love the Lord your God with all your heart, soul, mind and strength" is a command. But it is also an invitation. It is the way into life's deepest purpose. It is the way into life's deepest delight. It is how we live today

6. See John 15:14–15.

in the light of what is coming. It is how we get ready for "commencement."

Joy Unspeakable

I mentioned in chapter 19 a particularly moving performance of Mozart's *Requiem* when, at the conclusion, the audience sat stunned for an unusually long time before erupting in applause. Though I suspect that many in the concert hall did not know what to make of that moment just after the performance ended, I rejoiced that in a small way I did. I knew that we were stunned because we had come to the concert expecting to hear good music and had instead been visited by God. I was glad that I knew whom to thank for the event, and that the Person was big enough and worthy enough to receive the extravagance of my praise. And I was also thankful that I did not have to worry, as so many do after a transcendent musical experience, about losing the experience. For, though the *Requiem* happened in real time, and its impact began to fade almost immediately, the transcendent Person who gave us that moment did not fade away, and never will. He whispered to me, in effect, "You thought that was good? You just wait. That was glory—but glory a thousand steps removed from the beauty you will know when you see me face to face."

At the very end of *The Last Battle*, the final book in his *Chronicles of Narnia*, C. S. Lewis's young characters make a startling discovery. They suddenly realize that what they had thought had been a customary, temporary withdrawal into Narnia from England, was in fact something much more permanent. The great lion Aslan, who represents Christ in the stories, speaks:

> "You do not yet look so happy as I mean you to be."

> Lucy said, "We're so afraid of being sent away, Aslan. And you have sent us back into our own world so often."

> "No fear of that," said Aslan. "Have you not guessed?"

> Their hearts leaped and a wild hope rose within them.

> "There *was* a real railway accident," said Aslan softly. "Your father and mother and all of you are—as you used to call it in the Shadowlands—dead. The term is over: the holidays have begun. The dream has ended: this is the morning."

> And as He spoke He no longer looked to them like a lion; but the things that began to happen after that were so great and beautiful that I cannot write them. And for us this is the end of all the stories, and we can most truly say that they all lived happily ever after. But for them it was only the beginning of the real story. All their life in this world and all their adventures in Narnia had only been the cover and the title page: now at last they were beginning Chapter One of the Great Story which no one on earth has read: which goes on forever: in which every chapter is better than the one before.[7]

7. *The Last Battle* by C. S. Lewis. Copyright © C. S. Lewis Pte Ldt 1956. Extract reprinted by permission.

Questions
for Reflection and Discussion

1. Read 1 John 3:1–2. What will happen to us, if we are believers, when we see God? Why does seeing God have such an effect? Why will seeing God so clearly not terrify us?

2. How broad and deep is your enjoyment of God? What enhances it? What inhibits it?

3. Discuss the following statement. Is your connection with God more like a bad friendship or a good one?

   In a bad friendship we avoid each other, hide things from each other, perform for each other. But in a good friendship, we enjoy each other: we laugh together, do things together, tell silly jokes, share the things that interest us, go places together—we even waste time together.

4. Read through the quote from *The Last Battle* at the end of the chapter. How does Lewis address our fears that heaven will be a dreary place? When Lewis speaks of us living now in Shadowlands, does he mean that our lifework in this world does not matter? If not, what does he mean, and how does that motivate us to live life fully while we are still here?

He who has an ear, let him hear what the Spirit says to the churches. To him who overcomes I will give some of the hidden manna. I will also give him a white stone with a new name written on it, known only to him who receives it.

Revelation 2:17

21

Some Practical Parting Advice

What in practical terms do we do to figure out our purpose in the scheme of things? Let me try to summarize what I have been saying and end with a few practical suggestions.

First we have to cultivate the habit of thinking biblically about what is going on in and around us. We need, in other words, to believe and hold together in our minds the four Big Ideas we have been discussing: Creation, Fall, Redemption, and Consummation. We need to analyze and respond to our circumstances in the light of these ideas, an analysis that will keep us honest, hopeful, hard working, and realistic.

To believe in the Idea of Creation is to remember that our lives have a built-in purpose, even if we do not at the moment see what it is. To believe in Creation is also to see that life is filled with interesting possibilities—for there is no form of engagement with this good world (unless of course that form of engagement is twisted by sin) that is inherently less spiritual (and therefore less valuable) than any other.

But we must also believe in the tragic Idea of the Fall. If I really believe in the Fall, I will not be surprised when I do not get much time or opportunity to do the things I would love to do. If I really believe in the Fall, I will not be surprised when I experience frustration in my lifework, or when I discover ugly and debilitating attitudes in myself.

The Ideas of Redemption and Consummation bring hope to our struggles to know God and ourselves. When I remember that Christ gave his life to reconcile me forever to God, I find myself able to face and deal with the often-disturbing things about myself. And when I believe that the Second Adam, Christ, walks along the mountain path with me, when I discover that he knows the way because he has walked that path already, when I cling to the promise that he is ordering the twists and turns in the path (even the unpleasant ones) for my good, and when I experience his powerful and comforting presence, I find all the resources I need to keep climbing. And when I remember, or am given glimpses of, the view that awaits me at the top, I find additional energy for working hard (loving the Creator and his creation), letting go of false hopes (acknowledging the Fall), and loving people sacrificially (living out the promise of Redemption).

Remembering, of course, that we have yet to reach the summit (Consummation is still ahead), we should not demand full knowledge of God, other people, or ourselves or full satisfaction in the use of our gifts. Nevertheless we will not be wrong to look for some correlation between who we are and what we do, for we are good stewards when we seek to use the gifts God has given us.

Looking Upward, Inward, and Outward

But how in practical terms, beginning immediately, do we embark on the journey? We look upward, inward, and outward; and as we do this, we keep moving.

We look *upward* (responding to the primary call). We ask the Father, in other words, for direction. Acknowledging that "every good and perfect gift is from above, coming down from the Father of the heavenly lights,"[1] we repeatedly offer back to him the use of what he has bestowed. We live self-consciously as thankful and dependent stewards, poised to serve in whatever ways present themselves, refusing to hoard our lives.

We will also look *inward* (responding to the secondary call). We will ask, "What am I good at?" And, "What do I love to do?" Knowing that God gives us the desires of our hearts,[2] we will ask, "What draws out my interest?" Motivation is itself a gift—a call from the God who planted it there—a signpost of secondary calling. Though it is rarely possible in an imperfect world to pursue every interest, we should pursue what we can, as opportunity presents itself. And we should do this when we are young, before growing

1. James 1:17.
2. Ps. 37:4.

responsibility to family and friends obliges us to do only that which is feasible.

Personality and temperament inventories, such as Myers-Briggs, can help us with the inward look. We should not use them, however, as an excuse for selfishness ("I'm an intuitive type, so I don't really need to try to think anything through"). Nor should we see them as the last word. In my twenties I was "off the charts" extroverted; in my forties, I tested much more toward center. But such inventories can help us understand ourselves and be patient with the ways in which we differ from other people.

Honest discussions with trusted friends and colleagues can also help. I have been on a number of ministry team retreats during which each team member gets group input on his gifts. Always a little scary at first (what happens when it's my turn and no one has anything to say?!), they have always been illuminating and encouraging.

We will look *outward* as well (responding to the tertiary call). We will ask, "What needs in this fallen world grab my attention, and what opportunities and obligations present themselves to me?"[3] The Caller orders both our hearts and our circumstances, which means that if we look around with a heart to serve, we will invariably find something worth doing that resonates with who we are.

Moving Forward

Above all, we will *keep moving*. In other words, we mustn't just look up, in, and out; we must act. Someone has wisely said,

3. Gordon Smith highlights this aspect of the "outward look" in *Courage and Calling* (Downers Grove, IL: InterVarsity, 1999).

"You cannot steer a ship that isn't moving." The rudder needs to have water flowing past it if its movement is to affect the direction of the boat.

I am not advocating frenzy. But I am calling us away from the sort of introspection that stops us dead in the water. There is always something worthwhile to do—always someone to love. Press on. Don't bury your talent—however insignificant you may consider it to be. Do whatever is obviously obedient today. Do it even when you cannot fully figure out or clean up your motives—Jesus died to cleanse our hearts. Leave the big picture in God's hands and move out.

And never forget, as you make your way along the path to the summit, that calling is from a Person. It isn't essentially about doing. It is at heart about knowing—about knowing the magnificent and kind Person in whom "we live and move and have our being."[4] He is full of surprises; there is no way we can predict with certainty what course our lives will take. But he is also full of wisdom and love. The One who orders our days and knows our names gave his life for us. He saw his whole "career" crash in ruins—he lost his friends, his clout, his clothes, and, above all, his Father—in order to open his home and himself safely to us. And so, no matter what unfolds, we have nothing to fear, and we have a future of joy-filled discovery that defies imagination:

> What, then, shall we say in response to this? If God is for us, who can be against us? He who did not spare his own Son, but gave him up for us all—how will he not also, along with him, graciously give us all things?[5]

4. Acts 17:28.
5. Rom. 8:31–32.

Questions
for Discussion and Reflection

1. Take some time to read through the "Pilgrims on the Trail" stories in the appendix. Which of these stories resonates with particular force? Why? How is your story similar to it? How is it different? What principles apply to both?

2. Analyze your "story" in the light of the Big Ideas in this book: Creation, Fall, Redemption, and Consummation. Which of these ideas has held the least prominence in your way of thinking and behavior? With what effect? Which has held the most prominence? With what effect? How might holding all four ideas together with greater evenness make your quest for identity and purpose easier?

3. If you are in a group, share stories about your career and identity pilgrimage. Be honest—sharing things you understand and things you do not. Talk about your fallenness and about the Redeemer's work.

4. What are the three "looks" described in this chapter? What do you see as you look in each of these directions?

5. We have seen that "you cannot steer a ship that isn't moving." How are you moving today?

6. Read Romans 8:31–32 and turn it into a prayer of confident thanksgiving about your future.

Show me your ways, O Lord, teach me your paths;
guide me in your truth and teach me, for you are
God my Savior, and my hope is in you all day long.

Psalm 25:4-5

Pilgrims on the Trail

have chosen in this appendix to pass along a number of personal stories, portions of which have already appeared. All of them were told during public worship by friends and members of Emmanuel Presbyterian Church, where I serve as minister on Manhattan's Upper West Side. The presenters are all in their twenties, that season in life in which the questions of identity and purpose strike with particular ferocity. I have changed the names and some details to guard each person's privacy. My aim is to illustrate how the principles we have been discussing work themselves out in actual experience.

John's Story

"John" was a law student when he told us his story. He speaks vividly of the grip that succeeding in his chosen career has had on him. His terror at the prospect of academic (and career) failure is common, and it underscores how elusive success can be and how foolish it is, therefore, to bank on it. We must learn that we do not control the outcome of our efforts; only the Person who calls us does. Peace of mind in the pursuit of secondary calling comes to us only when faithfulness, rather than success or control, is our priority. John's story also reminds us of how good the Caller's intentions are—even when his methods are not comfortable. His principal aim is never to make us miserable, but he will allow our substitute gods to make us miserable if that is what it takes to bring us home to himself (that is, to primary calling). It is reassuring to be reminded that God will not, in the end, permit our often bad and destructive priorities to win the day. Here is John's story.

Countless times I've prayed something to the effect of, "God, help me grow in my faith," or, "Make yourself more real to me." I never quite knew by what means God would increase my faith. And I certainly never knew how much fright and pain could be associated with this process until a few months ago when my computer crashed. I had spent well over 300 hours writing outlines, case briefs, and notes. It was all in my computer. And none of it was backed up. I'm a first-year law student, and as you may know, law students' notes can be vital to their success. And first-year grades can be crucial to the sort of job you end up getting when you graduate. Bad first-year grades can get you off to a bumpy start in your legal career.

So I was sitting in class and I took out my trusty laptop and turned it on. The screen showed one of those error messages with all those letters and numbers that no one ever understands. They might as well just have shown one of those sad faces on the screen with a message saying, "You're in trouble, pal." You could tell that I was in real trouble because I started talking to my computer as though it was a pet dog.

My heart was throbbing and my body went numb. I think "desperately afraid" accurately describes how I felt at that point. Desperately afraid of what? Desperately afraid of flunking my exams and possibly flunking out of school, of not getting a "good" job, of not being in control over what was happening. I was also angry. Angry with a God who, claiming to love me, would do something that seemed so cruel. God could have been one of two things at that point: at best, he was a self-indulgent prankster; or at worst, he was a vindictive enemy.

When (overwhelmed with fear and anger) I called my mother to let her know what had happened, I unloaded a heap of screams, cries, and curses. At some point during my rant, my mother interrupted me and said, "Let's pray together. God can help you." To which I could only respond, "God! How can God help me! Why would he help me? He's the one who did this to me! Do you understand what's happened? My life is in that computer, and now everything is gone. Gone! There's nothing God can do!"

After I got off the phone with my mother, I sat at my desk and cried out to God, tears streaming down my face, "Why are you doing this to me? I hate what you're doing to me! If you really love me, show me that you do, because I just don't believe you right now." For all I knew my files had been wiped out. I couldn't remember the last time God seemed so terrifyingly silent.

Well, surprisingly, I got my files back. The tech guy at school somehow retrieved them for me. I thought it was a miracle at the time. But then again, you're looking at a guy who sometimes has trouble even turning on a computer, so maybe that doesn't say an awful lot. But if there is a miracle at all in this story, it can be found in the horrifying things I discovered about myself and the comforting things I learned about God.

About myself: that spiritual meltdown over the phone with my mother shows very clearly just how weak and fickle my faith in God is. It took the loss of something I valued greatly before I realized that I just didn't love or trust God as much as I thought I did. I felt so much more loving toward God when things were going along smoothly. But I sure loved and trusted him a lot less when I stood to lose those things I valued most. The fact is that my belief in God many times fluctuates with my personal circumstances. When God acts contrary to my intentions or preconceptions, I sometimes wish I could throw him overboard, so to speak, so that I could navigate my life as I'd like. This makes me a spiritual phony in a very real sense.

God managed to show his love for me in a very funny way. When I wondered why God had put me through this ordeal, I think he answered me quite clearly after the wreckage was cleared away. God seemed to say, "I knew all along just how weak your faith was. But you had no idea. You knew abstractly that my love for you doesn't at all depend on what you're capable of. This trial let you see more concretely that I love you despite your weaknesses, that I love you as if you have no flaws. My Son Jesus has made you perfect in my eyes. Your computer crashed so that you could see these things. And aren't you glad it happened?"

No way! But I couldn't imagine a better way of having learned these things.

Obviously, there is nothing that feels very tender or nurturing about experiencing difficulties. No! What God uses to show his love for us sometimes causes many tears, much fright, and much hurt. Growing closer to God, the thing a Christian wants most, is wrought with something people want least: pain. In addition to computer crashes, these include breakups, pulling all-nighters studying for multiple exams, experiencing the loss of a loved one, losing a job, or drowning inexplicably in depression. As C. S. Lewis points out, God was like a surgeon or dentist who could only make me better by first causing me pain. Like a surgeon, God operates with a very definite purpose in mind, though it is a purpose that we seldom can understand. But that purpose is always motivated by his love for us.

To be honest, part of me is still afraid of how God will answer my prayers for him to strengthen my faith. But now I have a better idea of who God is. And I trust him more. I trust his purposes more. I realize that I've got too many broken things within me, like doubts, insecurities, and selfish tendencies, that he still needs to fix. You've probably heard the verse "God disciplines those he loves." And I know he loves me far too much to let me go on as I am now.

If you're going through a difficulty now, believe, despite your feelings, that God loves you. Know that he will never leave you. He may seem silent, but he is the God who is there. He is close beside us. And he always will be.

Samantha's Story

"*Samantha*" *tells of losing her purpose and innocence during her undergraduate years at music school. Her story reminds us that neither a loving faith-filled home nor strong talent will automatically give us meaning or satisfaction, especially as we make our way through the college years and into independence. Our background and gifts (regardless of how we feel about them) may guide us, especially when we are young. But they do not define us—a fact that becomes clearer to us as we get older. They are rather the raw material out of which God shapes us. To put it another way, they are the "setting" in which we find ourselves as we learn how to love God and others.*

Samantha's story is in many ways typical and reminds us that discerning our secondary calling is not always easy, for at least two reasons: (1) Our limited and fallen world (the world still awaiting the great consummation) often does not provide a venue for the satisfactory expression of our particular gifts (to love piano and to be very talented at it do not necessarily fit us easily into the goals of a conservatory education); (2) Guilt because of bad moral decisions can afflict us so deeply that we can barely use our gifts at all.

Samantha's story reminds us that commitment to the church is an important part of inward healing and direction. And Samantha's story reminds us, finally, that God will often use the traumas associated with figuring out our secondary calling to bring us closer to himself (that is, to the primary call). Here is Samantha's story.

I remember, around the time of my graduation in 1999, bumping into one of my professors in the elevator. She told me graduation from college is the beginning, a commencement for many new things to come. Though her intention was good, this idea of a new beginning bothered me greatly because I was ready to fold my life and call it quits. I was tired of fruitlessly playing the piano; I was on the verge of breaking up with my boyfriend of many years. At that moment in my life, I felt my dreams were shattered and there was nothing more to live for.

My life did not end there as I had hoped, but continued on. Instead of plowing headlong into grad school like the rest of my peers, I decided, thanks to my parents' urging, to take the year off to practice piano and improve piano technique with a special coach who lived in New York. "Beginning anew" seemed highly unlikely since I would be trapped for another year in this city of shattered dreams. Countless mornings during that year off I awoke with pangs of emptiness that I had never previously known.

I had so much time on my hands. There were no classes to go to; no performances lined up; no teachers to please; no Christian fellowship group to plan for. I wasn't busy anymore. And it's a terrible thing not to be busy in New York. Though the days seemed to run seamlessly from one to another, I forced myself to practice daily and somehow managed to do so out of habit and duty. I went to my piano lessons begrudgingly; I had lost all desire and motivation to play.

During the vast amounts of time I had to myself, I began to question my life choices. I questioned my decision to go to a conservatory. Wouldn't I have been much happier meeting normal friends and normal teachers at a normal university? What kind of job could I now get with a piano performance degree?

I also looked back into my past relationships and despaired over the choices I had made. Much worse than this feeling of emptiness and meaninglessness to life, there were these memories, like stains that I could not get rid of. I kept remembering all the times I had compromised my values and beliefs, rebelled and disobeyed my parents; how I hid my faith in subtle and not so subtle ways to please my teachers, friends, and significant others; how I ruthlessly pursued my own pleasures and dreams during college. Rub as hard I tried, I could not get rid of these thoughts. In fact, these memories followed me into the subway, onto the streets, into my practice room. Like a shadow, the remembrance of all my misdeeds trailed behind, next to, in front of me, wherever I went. I couldn't seem to run away from it; couldn't erase it.

I scoured the Bible for some comfort at this time. It's surprising how many passages describe the wrath of God and his anger over the faithlessness of Israel. I would flip randomly to a page, and his angry words seared me. I was impure, defiled, and tainted. The Lord abhorred my sins because he is perfect, and these sins separated me from his love. As a result, the sins plagued me with a guilty conscience, remorse, and regret. I was being convicted of the weight and gravity of sin.

September of that year, I had crawled into Redeemer Church[1] with an impulse to get involved and, I quickly plugged in to a home fellowship group. I'd grown up in a Christian home, but the years of wandering and hopping through churches in college left me quite the stranger in the house of God. I don't think I shared much about my inner struggles with the people in my fellowship group, though they must have seen how lost

1. Redeemer Presbyterian Church is the leader in a movement of churches that sparked the founding of Emmanuel.

I was. They loved me nonetheless—with glowing smiles and hugs, kind gestures, great food, fun games—and most importantly I caught a glimmer of Jesus' love for me.

I'm thankful for the year off because I know it was God who made me see the deep stains, the dark shadows, and the great weight of my wrongs. He was disciplining me and making me taste and experience life without Jesus . . . hollow and empty, aimless and purposeless, alone and without hope. In retrospect, I see how in that year, God used a burnt-out pianist and wayward Christian such as myself to bring my piano teacher to church. She received Christ as Savior and Lord of her life that year.

Since then, God has been slowly and carefully restoring my relationship with him. He has been teaching me through the Bible and through my brothers and sisters here in church that I am loved and accepted and that my past mistakes and poor choices have been wiped clean by the blood of Jesus. I praise him for the hope I now have for the future as I pursue a teaching degree at Columbia Teachers College. I thank God for making every morning a new day in which I can drink deeply from his promises. Most importantly, I'm thankful for a new love relationship. This sacred covenant of love and faithfulness, this knowledge of being loved by God so completely, despite my sins, fills me with joy and meaning. Though I still sometimes struggle with despair, I cling to the truth that Jesus forgives and saves me from my sins. In Jesus alone, I rest my hope.

Geoffrey's Story

"Geoffrey's" story tells largely of God's calling into the church. Geoffrey challenges our consumer mindset by telling us of his discovery that pursuing God in isolation from

God's people is disobedient. He also hints at the notion we developed in chapter 10 that isolation inhibits self-discovery (secondary calling) because it makes it easier to be dishonest about ourselves. Here is Geoffrey's story.

I've always listened to other people's testimonies in awe—how through adversity, trials, and tribulations they triumphed. So what's my story? I moved to New York from California five years ago after I graduated from college to start as an analyst in one of the investment banks. The city is a lonely place, and you start to ask the big questions. About two months into the job, at the company cafeteria, I bumped into an old friend from high school. Turns out, he was also working at the firm, in another division. We had lost touch during college, so over the following weeks, we renewed our friendship.

One Friday afternoon, a few months later, he asked if I wanted to attend church with him. I didn't really know he was Christian. As my friend, he had tremendous credibility built up over time—he was a fun, smart person I liked to hang out with and respected in every other regard—so why not? I fancied myself being intellectually open minded and "tolerant." So I went to church with him . . . then gradually started going to church more on my own . . . then actually started to read the Bible on its own terms. About three years ago, I finally came to accept Jesus as my Savior. Great.

But here's the problem, and here's where things get interesting. I always had this idea that being saved would be a "Eureka!" moment—like in high school chemistry when you learn about energy levels in an atom. Conversion was a state change or a new energy level—some sort of switch. All of a sudden, magic pixie dust is sprinkled on you and you become a perfect human being, free from the messiness of everyday life.

But this wasn't what happened.

Life stays messy. I am still deeply flawed. There are a million ways that I fail. My friends probably know best the times when I let them down or do hurtful things to others—my numerous daily acts of rebellion against God's love.

Among these numerous personal failings and acts of rebellion was the fact that I never got baptized or joined a church as a member. It might seem strange to include not joining a church among a list of rotten things that we do, but it is. It's a really rude thing that we do to God.

What were my reasons? First, I was just too busy to get baptized. I just procrastinated on it. Second, why join a church as a member? Two years ago, I started coming to Emmanuel. I took the membership class to deepen my knowledge about the Christian faith and theology, but never signed aboard as a member. I couldn't really do it. Why would I want some other people telling me how to live my life? Why would I want to do that? First, hey, it's between me and Jesus. Church is not filled with perfect angelic people. (I mean, *I'm* here, right?) Why do I want to be accountable or follow guidance from imperfect people?

But about six months ago, something started to dawn on me. I had turned into a church consumer. Show up, listen to the sermon, maybe stay afterwards for coffee hour to say hi to people. It was about me, me, me. What religious warm fuzzies could I get from church? What sort of fun goody bag of intellectual ideas could I take away from the service? I was just a consumer—might as well be at a mall shopping. Is this how Christ, my Savior, Lord, and Friend would want me to relate to his church? Probably not. I started to realize that I have to trust God in all facets of my life. Not getting baptized or joining a church was an act of rebellion against him.

This really started to weigh heavily on me. It was intellectually and spiritually dishonest. This act of rebellion was linked to my fear of accountability. For all the million ways that I fail, I didn't want to be accountable to a community or to other people. Christ, though, makes us accountable to him. Through grace he forgives us and draws us to be a community. That's the beauty of it. It has taken me a while to figure out.

So this is where I am—really appreciative and grateful for his grace. I'm tired of rebelling. So I'm just taking the next step and making it more honest.

Ying's Story

We end with "Ying's" remarkable story because it draws together much of what we have discussed in the book. Her story affirms the inherent holiness of all legitimate callings—in this case, music (remember the Big Idea of Creation?)—while also demonstrating how readily we can pervert our callings (the Fall). Ying's story also shows the Redeemer at work (Redemption), sorting out primary and secondary calling, drawing her back to himself and into authentic Christian community (primary calling is not simply to God but also to God's people), and then giving back to Ying that which she had largely lost (a taste of heaven—Consummation). With that return has come also a sense of mission (another aspect of Redemption) beautifully suited to her own opportunities and gifts. She has discovered and joined in the Caller's invitation to her musical friends. Here is Ying's story.

The story I have to tell today is about how God used the gift of music to pursue me and to draw me toward himself.

I came to New York City seven years ago at the age of seventeen to study classical piano at the Juilliard School of Music. At once, I loved it all and saturated myself with music. I thrust myself into my studies, practicing, learning, going to concerts, and thinking about the nature of the art. For this lonely, searching young girl, music seemed to represent the best of humanity and provide the most meaning and integrity in a cold and empty world. To identify with beauty and truth in music then felt to me a much more tangible and fulfilling spiritual experience than any I had growing up in the church. So I pursued it with all that I had. It became my religion, my mode of thinking, and my value system. It was not difficult to find others at Juilliard and in New York City who identified with music in the same way. In a culture where superficiality and senselessness are prevalent, it was not difficult to justify the fervor and enthusiasm with which my friends and I devoted ourselves to the religion of Art.

With this sort of dedication, I met with success and accomplishment during my time at school. The praise I received caused me to build my identity further on music, and I soon made it into an idol that ruled me. All the while, the Lord Jesus, whom I had accepted into my heart at the age of six, waited patiently. Deep down I knew that the faith I had in him was calling me to examine why I was worshiping something else. Like a good "artist/intellectual," I wore the face of doubt earnestly, and used it as a mask for the pride that became more and more puffed up by achievement and selfishness. I had felt, for the most part, misunderstood growing up in the church, and now that I had found meaning and identity in

Art, my Christian faith and my vocation as a musician were at direct odds. I remember one vivid moment attending a large Christian worship service hearing thousands praise God, and feeling entirely isolated and absolutely unable to hand over Lordship of my life to Jesus.

But God did not stop pursuing me in his love. He used people, mainly, to show me that what I thirsted for in my musical pursuits could only be found in relationship, and relationship based on Christ. A Christian classmate at Juilliard, whom I had scoffed at for a long while for being deficient in her devotion to Art, unbeknownst to me, started praying that we would have fellowship together. This friendship became a source of solace to me, while the ties I had formed with others, based on achievement and worldly accomplishment, were showing themselves to be tenuous, self-serving, and disappointing.

At the same time, to borrow a phrase from C. S. Lewis speaking of George MacDonald's writing, God "baptized my imagination." By his grace and good pleasure, my artistic sensibilities were being led into the realm of *his* creation, away from man-exalting craft. Using the words of the great Christian writer J. R. R. Tolkien, my experience of color, sound, language, and beauty were brought across a threshold from darkness to light. My understanding and imagination for truth and beauty were being revived and redeemed, slowly but surely. Through reading *The Lord of the Rings*, primarily, I had tasted of the beauty of the truth of Christ, and I could never go back to worshipping a dead and wooden god.

The next several years in New York bring me here now, to the present. They have been an incredible journey, all about God's faithfulness and delight in bringing this musician and human being more and more into the realm of the Kingdom of his people. Emmanuel Presbyterian Church has become a home where as a Christian and musician I have found affirmation, acceptance, and healing, I'm supported by a community that encourages me to use my musical gifts in the freedom and joy with which our Father has given them. The church has given me a context for the things I *need* to express as a human being, and the Kingdom of God has shown me the truths that must be expressed to the world.

The music I now play says, "In the love of God through Christ do all things hold together. In the brokenness of humanity, including the very musicians who play music, is music beautiful." . . .

Through the leading of the Holy Spirit, and in gratefulness for what he has done for us, some of the musicians here at Emmanuel and I had a vision to extend this community, and the healing it can bring, to the many colleagues we have in our spheres of musical influence. That is how we came up with the Elbereth Chamber Music Series.[2] We simply wanted to bring beautiful music to this community, in the church, in this neighborhood, in order to show God's pleasure and love for musicians and music. Through this simple act, we hoped to create a living testament and example to struggling young instrumentalists out there, often unappreciated, doubtful of their gifts, and unable to find opportunities to use their talents.

Elbereth's first concert was two Sundays ago. . . . I think of one performer, whom I had previously only known as withdrawn and shy, now lit up and joyful when I see her, somehow

2. Elbereth was a series of chamber music concerts offered free of charge over the course of a year to our church family and to the public. The aims were: (1) to demonstrate God's grace and beauty both in the music itself and in the free offering of it; and (2) to draw fellow musicians, many of whom were not themselves believers, into the orbit of the church.

brought into his freedom and fellowship through the time we spent playing music together. The first concert was marked with a sheer, God-given joy in playing together, which so often is tragically absent in professional situations.

I have faith that God will continue to be faithful in my life, and specifically that he will be faithful to the vision of the Elbereth Chamber Music Series. For this musician, this kind of embrace from the church has spoken volumes of God's loving presence often unsaid in sermons. This embrace from the church is much needed in our time.

Educated at Harvard University and Westminster Theological Seminary, Charles Drew has served churches in university communities for nearly thirty years and is presently the senior minister of Emmanuel Presbyterian Church near Columbia University in Manhattan. He is the author of *The Ancient Love Song: Finding Christ in the Old Testament* and *A Public Faith: Bringing Personal Faith to Public Issues*. He lives with his wife, Jean, in Riverdale, New York.